GULLIBLE'S TRAVELS

Also by Jim McAllister

Ungifted

The Journey

Jim McAllister's Encyclopaedia of Fighting Arts

You Can't Judge a Book...

GULLIBLE'S TRAVELS

Jim McAllister

First published in Great Britain by Jim McAllister

Copyright © Jim McAllister 2023

Cover design and layout by Andy Bowden
Cover Illustration by Rev Max Blake
Back cover background: © Shutterstock

ISBN (Paperback): 9798393640767

Contents

A Tom Pepper

I knew Jim way back when I was about 17 years old, when I used to attend a Taekwondo class in the United Services club in Stanford le Hope, although I only knew him, to say "hello".

In 2018, our paths crossed again, we said that we would meet up, I thought as friends -for coffee and a catch up. I had followed him over the years (with his martial arts) and was fascinated as to where he was now. We had a coffee in his clinic and then a few more coffees, a dinner (the tight so and so) we went to Harvester in Rayleigh as he had vouchers (buy one get one free lol, he knew how to treat a girl) a day's outing to a car show in Maldon and a visit to see my brother Brian in St Osyth, as he also knew Brian through Karate.

We got on really well and decided to see each other but only on a casual basis. I thought he came across as a shy, sensitive but very funny witty man. He intrigued me with all the stories that he told me and unfortunate adventures he had with buying and selling. I thought no one could be that unfortunate or unlucky, I thought he must be a Tom Pepper (Story teller)

Laugh out loud (as they say in texting language) I have now been with Jim for 3 years and can tell you that all the stories of being scammed, ripped off on either buying, selling items, cars and selling/renting properties not forgetting the situations he has had on his boat -are all true. I have witnessed all and can understand if no one believes them.

As for him being a shy and sensitive man as I thought, I couldn't have been more wrong. I watched him in one of his Tuesday night Kick-boxing classes and he certainly wasn't shy or sensitive, he was really quite spiteful and nasty, when demonstrating techniques on his poor students.

As for Jim's Martial Arts, he has travelled to many countries learning, training and taking classes and is respected by a lot of people high in their ranks. He is now an eighth Dan and is amazing to watch. He has written four books and has just finished writing syllabuses on four weapons, which has taken time and effort. He has great tenacity and intelligence. I do not think that Jim's students realise how lucky they are to have him as their Sensei.

Jim writes with 100% honesty, nothing is exaggerated.

So over to you Jim

Jacqui Simmonds

Being Gullible

I have always had ambitions and ideas of becoming Richard Branson or Alan Sugar; unfortunately I have not the business brain. I am very gullible and believe everything people tell me, as it will unfold in this book.

As long as I can remember I have always tried to be an entertainer and entrepreneur, this was brought about by the fact that I was an only child for several years, where I was encouraged to sing and entertain my relatives. In my performance I would charge a penny for a song. "Oh my Papa" was tuppence. Unfortunately as I got older my selling skills got overtaken by my buying; this coupled with my gullible nature probably explains why I am always skint.

As a child we went on holiday, which was always to Biggleswade or Jaywick Sands. I would spend my holiday money before we arrived.

My next realisation of being a bad business person was becoming friends with Billy Fisher. Bill was a wild boy who grew up to be an infamous wheeler dealer in the area. I would swap comics, cigarette cards and stamps, with Bill who would persuade me to swap my classic comics and cig cards (that were in pristine condition) and were worth much more than his old and tatty ones with his.

Another aspect which endorses my gullibility and impulse was when I used to go to school jumble sales, I would return home with a book that had been scribbled on or pages missing or toys that would not work.

My first involvement buying and selling happened later in life, when a friend of my dads, who he worked with, used to bring in various goods to the house with no questions asked as to where they came from. I used this opportunity to make some extra cash. I would take to work various items that he had brought around. I made a small profit which I used to purchase some bits for myself. This lasted a short while until my Dad showed his disapproval.

My next experience in the buying and selling game was when one of my students, who will remain nameless, bought some Black & Decker goods to the class one night, which he obtained from a cousin of his, again I seized the opportunity to make some extra cash by taking some to work and selling them. Once again most of the profit went into buying stuff for me.

This went on for a couple of years until I had a close shave. Somebody asked me at work if I could get them any goods that would be suitable for a retirement home that he and his wife owned. I had been given a batch of clocks from my friend, so I took them to work and offered them to Fred who declined the offer saying most old people would not find use for them.

After finishing my late shift, I loaded my car with two black sacks of clocks, ready to return to my friend who I was meeting in the Robinson Crusoe pub. Whilst driving up Hogg Lane in Grays, I got flagged down by a policeman and he climbed into the car telling me to chase a car in front. He apologised, but didn't realise he was holding two sacks of stolen clocks. When reaching the end of the road, he got out, after spotting who we were chasing and thanked me and carefully placed the sacks back on the seat. When meeting up with my friend and explaining what had happened, someone cracked a joke that I could have got TIME!

I have always been interested and fascinated with motor bikes.

My parents were overprotective and would not allow me to have one, when all my friends had motorbikes or scooters. My mum rode a moped (Autovap) and eventually

conceded and let me have hers. This was not very cool but I did try to jazz it up with streamers. My dad later agreed for me to have a motorbike combination. It was legal to ride a large capacity motorbike with a sidecar.

I bought my first motorbike combination. It was a 650cc BSA Goldenflash with a huge sidecar. I immediately took the huge side car off and replaced it with a small box with paving slabs in it.

I took out my first HP contract for £35 and the repayments would have been ten shillings a month. After a year, I wanted to upgrade it. My dad and I went to Pride & Clarks in London to part exchange it for a BMW Motorcycle, they offered me £10 part exchange to which my dad lost his temper and called them Pride & Sharks. So I decided to keep the motorbike and get it serviced, unfortunately just before arriving home at Chadwell St Mary the motorbike back fired outside Chadwell Cemetery and caught on fire, not only the motorbike but the road as well! As I had taken out the cheapest insurance which was just a third party. I had to continue my payments with no motorbike.

My next motorbike that I bought was a solo 250cc BSA C15, I again bought this on HP. My dad signed for it thinking I had finished HP repayment on the other one.

On Sunday mornings I would polish my motorbike (It was traditional for people to polish and clean motorbikes) especially the chrome prior to going to the motorbike cafes in the afternoon.

This particular Sunday I decided to pop up to the garage and fill up with petrol before lunch. I shouted to my mum that I wouldn't be long-I was going to the garage, to which she replied "Put your crash helmet on". This was not a legal requirement at the time, I didn't.

The next thing I remember was waking up in Old Church hospital, with a broken arm and fractured skull.

What had happened was I had gone round the corner too fast and hit a lamp post; I was rushed to Orsett hospital where they decided to transfer me to Old Church hospital. On the way, the ambulance broke down so had to be transferred to another and when arriving had to undergo surgery. My poor parents, this must have been their worst nightmare. The irony of this story was on the Saturday before the accident, I had gone to Romford market with my friend Ronnie Seaman and stole a St Christopher pendant which is supposed to be the patron saint of travel. I now had no motorbikes but was paying for two.

After that I went back to combinations which I bought off my friend, a Triumph T110 with a bullet fairing and a bullet side-car.

I then went onto cars until some years later when I worked at Murco I bought a Suzuki 125 off a person who worked with my dad. The bike was in pristine condition as he had never ridden it. It had a unique sound, which is relevant to the story. I only used the bike to go back and forth from my house in Grays then to work (West Thurrock). I only mentioned this because I never took the ignition key out of the bike as it was only left outside my house or outside my office.

One evening after work, I called in the local osteopath, Ken Metson as I had a bad back at the time. When I came out my bike was missing and I realised I had left the ignition key in, and my crash helmet on the seat (a habit that I had) I was annoyed with myself as much as I was annoyed with the person who had stolen my bike.

I walked home via the Civic Hall as I knew lots of bikers hung around there. I came home to no avail because I had no bike and I was upset with myself.

A week or so later, when I received a phone call from Mick Pickard, my supervisor at Murco who lived in Tilbury next to a multi storey car park. He was off sick at the time recovering from a hernia operation, asking me if I had my bike stolen, the reason being, he recognised the unique sound of the bike being ridden by a joy rider, up and down the car park. Although the bike had been painted black, the person who stole it had left the original number plates on it. Mick called the police and I drove down there like a bat out of hell. The police arrested the heavily tattooed thief and took him to the police station. I followed on and when I got to the police station he was being questioned on one side of the counter while I was standing in reception on the other side. I was ok, fairly calm until he stuck a finger up at me, I did no more than jump over the counter and grabbed him. The police restrained me and now instead of being the victim, I was given a caution!

Analogies, anyone who knows me will endorse the fact I use a lot of analogies when explaining a situation, especially when teaching martial arts. My cousin Vic says I'm the analogy king but others may call me an analogy bore.

The analogy I'm going to use to give a back drop of this particular aspect of my life are relating to ingredients. To get optimum results in anything one needs all the ingredients, for example a cake would not taste as good if an ingredient was left out, not dissimilar to an orchestra leaving out what often appears as an insignificant member, such as the percussion with the triangle in a piece of classical music.

On the other side of the coin, a champion sportsman needs all the ingredients to become top of his field, fitness, timing, strength, focus and determination.

To perform a technique, karate for example, one needs distance, timing, relaxation and tension, hip rotation again to get optimum results.

Nervous breakdowns, violent actions, strokes and heart attacks could also be attributed to numerous factors.

"The last straw" is often used to describe a situation when numerous things have taken place before the possible explosion takes place.

A well known film "Falling Down" starring Michael Douglas portrays the situation very well.

What on earth has this to do with the subject which I'm going to write about, my adventures or misadventures over the next few chapters.

I thought I should describe a bit about my personality and then it may be easier to understand why I did or do what may appear foolish, impulsive or adventurous.

I have all the ingredients to either make mistakes or make a fortune. Firstly, I trust people, good and bad you may ask. I believe adverts and what people say. I am spontaneous and have no patience when it comes to either doing or buying.

I love buying things not only for myself but for other people. I take chances, but as the saying goes, "A fool and his money are soon parted".

Am I gullible or is it that I just trust people? I am also a bit conceited, which makes me think people I know would not catch me "because they like me". Big mistake, as I have been caught by friends or those who I thought were friends.

So I have given a bit of a backdrop of why I have done things, I'll now write why I was possibly built that way.

My theory is that we inherit lots of traits from our parents.

We know that physical aspects such as hair, colour, height and facial features can be recognised by looking at our parents.

I do get a bit confused when people looking at a day old baby say things like "oh doesn't he or she look like the dad" perhaps this was said by the mums' family trying to confirm he is the dad.

Personality traits, such as humour, temper etc., can also be linked to the parents.

We don't always like what we have inherited and try to change the bits we don't want. Of course we have our own bits and circumstances, lifestyle can alter our personality a great amount.

"But" we have inherited parental traits that we can not alter, in marriage this often gets thrown in when arguing, you are getting like your mother or you are just like your father are common phrases used.

I am going to write a bit about my mum and dad to perhaps find out why I am the way I am sorry Mum and Dad, you were the best parents anyone could have had. I am sure my children could write one or two things about me.

Good luck when writing the Eulogy

Mum

My mum was a caring, loving lady who could cook, bake and make a cosy home wherever we moved to, to which, was a lot as we had council houses and to exchange was just a matter of putting and advert on the shop notice board or council offices, stating what you wanted and where you wanted and waited for someone to contact and see if it was what you wanted.

Mum was the shrewd one, always got a bargain, all my clothes were second hand, probably from jumble sales, you will grow into them was the phrase mum used to convince me that the shirt that the sleeves covered my hands would eventually fit. I don't think they would fit me now!

My first two wheeled bike had no crossbar and caused me to be ridiculed by all the boys in the street.

Mum's solution was to call it a French boys bike, which, in fairness did look different as the cross bar or the slope cross bar, had two tubes, it convinced me and the other boys.

Mum would stay up all night making clothes and later things for the school play that I would wear and I always

won the novelty hat competition at the Christmas party because of mum's imagination and "tenacity".

I inherited those traits form her

Later on in my childhood we would go on holiday to Birchington near Margate, I'll come back to that in dad's chapter. We had little money so the bucket and spade was all we had.

Mum had a game of bingo on the promenade while Colin (my brother), dad and I played on the beach. Mum came back with a football she had won. That was the start of what was to be a problem. Mum kept winning, a cricket set, a flask etc. This made our holiday, but mum got hooked on bingo

When returning home, mum had become addicted to bingo, another parent related trait. This in itself wasn't too bad as she would go once or twice a week until...

She won the nationals. I can't remember how much she won, but even though it was a three way share with my Nan and Aunt, she still had enough to treat all of us.

This was the downward spiral, as she became hooked and would go to bingo every opportunity, justifying it by saying I might get the big one again, she never did!

Mum stopped going to bingo when she moved to Clacton, and even when moving back to Dunton she never went again. Unfortunately a much bigger problem was to come.

Dad

My dad was a marine during the war and in fact drove a landing craft on Juno Beach on D Day.

Dad was incredibly strong, a trait I have partially inherited, gullibility which I have totally inherited and a vicious temper. Although I have snapped on a few occasions I generally keep it under control, this maybe as I have witnessed the damage it caused when Dad lost his, also my Martial Arts training could be a contributing factor.

Dad believed people, sounds familiar!

The reason we went to Birchington for our holiday was because the man in the fish shop convinced dad that his caravan which, he only let out to close friends and family, was the best one on the site and as dad was a good customer he could rent it.

I won't say it was small, but we all had to go to bed at the same time as the table had to come down for us all to have any sort of bed.

Dad also listened to people, his brother Harry was a know it all and a bragger, so dad would only buy tomatoes and potatoes to grow if Harry had done. Dad could have been a PTO in the marines, bought his own Bungalow and numerous other things, if he had not let his so-called friends talk him out of them.

When moving back to Dunton, dad became friends with Joe. Joe was pleasant enough and would take dad to France, the Booze Run.

Dad would say how good it was of Joe to drive and pay

for the trip. All dad was to do was give Joe his tobacco and drinks allowance. Of course what Joe was doing was selling the drinks and tobacco to all his neighbours, Mum cottoned on to this, as she was the shrewd one.

Dad enjoyed his trips and what Joe did, did not bother him, but to keep Mum happy he would bring her a bottle of wine/brandy back.

What dad didn't realise was giving mum a bottle was the start of her becoming an alcoholic!

To see my mum decline was one of the saddest things I have ever seen.

She went from a smart funny lady, brilliant Mum/Nan to a shadow of her former self.

So all the ingredients are there, those aspects of my life might explain a bit of why I have leaped before I looked. Been wise after the event, and only just realised that if it looks too good to be true, it probably isn't.

Here Goes

My Early Days

I suppose my early memories of being gullible or spendthrift was at Chadwell St Mary School, my first jumble sale experience. I took some bits that mum gave me, and spent some money. I came back with no money, a children's book with pages missing, a doily and something I had taken.

When I was nine years old we moved from Chadwell to Stifford Clays. I became friends with Billy Fisher. To talk about Billy would take a book to explain what he was like. Bill was part gypsy and had the gift of the gab. Later on in life he ran the snooker hall in Grays, sold bits at fetes, working men clubs, stole lead off roofs and eventually owned Fisher's Flower shop that resembled *Open all Hours*.

Bill could charm the birds out of the trees. He was a likeable rogue. He got me into trouble on more than one occasion. The only time my dad hit me was when he told me not to hang around with Billy, and found out I had. I would assist in his stealing, but unfortunately got caught.

My dad would bring home a classic comic, once a month,

a thick comic that would tell a story of one of the classic books such as William Tell or Robin Hood. I also had a collection of war stories, again all in good condition, Bill somehow would talk me into exchanging my comics for his. No prizes for guessing who got the better deal. Cigarette cards, stamps would also be swapped for inferior ones.

When my mum died I went to Bill's shop to order the flowers. I, knowing that Bill knew my mum, asked for a discount, Bill's answer was "Classic" "It's unlucky to discount flowers at a funeral", he said, I still chuckle at the answer – God Rest Bill.

They say hindsight is a wonderful thing, but the strange thing is I have enjoyed my life, on one hand I think I have been a bit unlucky with things I have bought or perhaps the timing, but I'll make a fortune when this book is published or "So I have been told".

Watches

I like buying things, love watches, and believe people, what does that conjure up? Disaster!

Someone said that all the watch sellers in Spain knew when Jim McAllister was going there, well it's not just in Spain that I have had the pleasure of relieving me of my money in exchange for a watch.

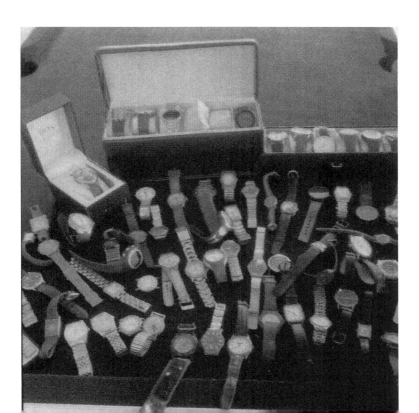

As a child, a watch was something you got as a birthday or Christmas present, usually a Timex.

I always wanted a square or oblong watch, Omega was the watch rich people wore. My Auntie Rhoda, had no children but lots of nephews and nieces, she was a kind and generous lady and would give all of the nephews and nieces either a Parker Pen or a watch with a date on for their 21st birthday. For some unknown reason this stopped by the time it was my 21st.

However, my mum and dad bought me an oblong Avia watch for my 21st birthday. I loved this watch and wore short sleeve shirts to show it off. This was until an incident occurred. I have written in depth of this in my autobiography *Ungifted* that when hitting someone in a fight, I broke the glass.

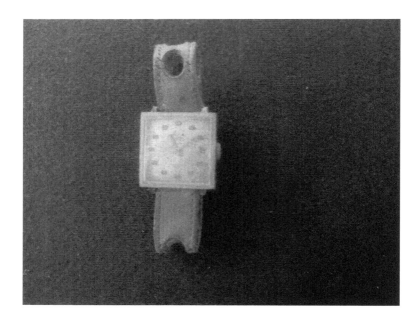

Again I listened to someone who recommended a horologist that worked from his home and would be able to repair it for me. A year later, after calling around his house every week, I got the watch back.

The irony of this watch story is that shortly after getting the treasured watch back I was involved in a road rage incident and was wearing the watch at the time, yes history repeated itself, I punched the driver, and yes you guessed it, broke the watch!!!!

One incident that should have flagged up a warning sign regarding watches was when I was on holiday in Italy. One of the excursions I went on was to the famous Rimoni market, on the coach going to the market the courier warned everyone that there was a lot fake watches and gold being sold by convincing Italians, knowing this, I was on my guard, I resisted all the watch sellers, well that was until one approached me with a real, genuine Omega, of course I knew it was a fake, but it looked like the genuine article. The seller was asking about £20 or the equivalent in Lira. I stood my ground, resisted the watch, I justified my not buying by explaining I had only £10 or equivalent on me, and to prove it I showed him the note. How he managed to exchange the note for the watch was amazing, I don't think Paul Daniels could have done it better.

But it did look good, so I wasn't too upset. When I got back on the coach the courier asked if we had a good time, everyone said yes then she asked did anyone buy gold or watches, no one answered. I looked out of the window sheepishly.

She must have known that at least one of the passengers had bought one, so she then asked if who bought one should look at their wrist. I gingerly looked at mine, a green band where the watch was prominent. A good job I learnt from this…

As I mentioned earlier, when I worked for Murco I used to sell various items, I thought myself as a bit of an Arthur Daley, and in fact Johnny Fisher nicknamed me Trotter!

One of the drivers who came into the depot approached me one day and said he had an idea that might help me make a few bob. I love spending money so making extra was handy. I used to stage concerts, Dances and of course Kickboxing shows, which I will talk about more in later chapters.

The driver knew I had lots of contacts and witnessed me wheeling and dealing so I was the ideal person to pass on this once in a lifetime opportunity.

He showed me a copy of GQ Magazine, a glossy magazine, and opened it to a page selling watches. Anyone who has read GQ knows that everything is expensive. Shirts, pens and wallets are all top names and prices.

The watches were of course very expensive. What the driver told me was that his brother in law was a rep for the watch company, and was allowed to keep the samples he showed the jewellers. What he was offering was if I was to buy twenty watches he would let me have them for a fraction of the retail price enabling me to put some on and still sell them for a third of the market price, of course being bitten more times than a zoo keeper I was sceptical.

I question the authenticity of the advert and he suggested I phone the company direct, the number was on the advert so, being, a bit more streetwise than I used to be, I phoned the company from my office, the well spoken lady that answered the phone, naming the company, confirmed the story I had been told thus prompting me to buy the watches before someone else did. I rushed home, gathered the money from every place I could, electric, savings and hall hire money came back and bought the watches. I immediately went out and bought a few copies of GQ, not easy to get in Grays at the time, but armed with watches and magazines I was off for the kill.

Amazingly I had no trouble selling the watches and made enough to buy one for myself.

One of my close friends Terry Griffiths, a street wise person who was the one who told me if it sounds too good to be true then it isn't – bought one.

Some weeks later he came to my house and I knew something was wrong. I am a bad judge of character but a sensitive person when something is not right. I wish the two would join up, well he was in a dilemma as should he tell me what he had experienced.

Terry had taken the watch to the jewellers not sure if it was a strap or battery, but asking the jeweller to value it, I think curiosity or insurance were possibly the reasons.

The jeweller said it was a nice watch, probably worth what he had paid for it but nowhere near, the price we were led to believe was the original price.

Of course it now seems obvious what the scam was, a group of people bought the cheapest watches, paid for the advert in GQ, and one of the consortium manned the phone.

Since then I have been approached several times when driving in nice cars, I have been told the scamming targets BMW and Mercedes drivers I had both.

Not every watch experience was bad; a good friend of mine, Big Gordon, a JCB driver extraordinaire retrieved a batch of top quality watches and kindly gave me one.

I recently purchased a Geekthink, a lovely looking watch, and wore it when going to my cousin's 70th birthday party, an opportunity to show off a bit I suppose. When booking into the hotel I was to stay in, I was in the lift when the doors went to close on an elderly lady. Having quite a good reaction I threw my arm out to stop the doors closing and the doors closed on my arm, well in fact smashed my treasured watch.

Saturday Newspapers

The newspapers on Saturdays always had lots of adverts, well at least the papers we had, probably the Daily Mirror. All sorts of ridiculous things would be advertised, X-Ray glasses, add height shoes (had I known I wasn't going to grow any taller, I should have bought them) Bull worker, how to defend yourself books showing a karate chop.

Believe it or not I did not buy any of these, well until I saw the advert for snow boots, worn by the Arctic explorers. Being in the scouts and preparing for a weekend camping at the Condovers in the winter, was too much of a temptation to resist.

They arrived in time to show off these boots at the camp, an added bonus was it was snowing, all the other lads had ordinary wellington boots. Looking both sceptical and envious of my white cloth knee length boots, the wellington donned scouts watched me show off the durability and practicality of buying authentic snow boots.

This was until I went back in the log cabin we were sleeping in, everyone's feet were cold but dry, mine was not only cold but soaking wet, as we had no phone either on the camp or at home, I could not get mum or dad to bring my old wellingtons, so I had to put plastic bags on my feet before putting on the boots, my snow boots were Snow Good!!!

Today's equivalent of Saturdays' bargains is eBay.

Disaster, especially with PayPal, everything looks bigger and better when advertising with a photo. This is often enhanced when a video clip is added.

I most recently bought special glass glue; coincidently I noticed a long crack on one of my car's windows. I then saw a video clip showing a car with an almost identical crack being invisibly mended by the super glass repairing kit. I immediately sent for a kit, when it arrived I followed the instructions by the letter (unlike what I normally do) after it looked no different! With an MOT due, I had to call auto glass for a new windscreen!

I would take too long to mention all the things I have bought that have not done what it says on the tin or arrived!

If a job needs welding, get it welded, not buy special glue that replaces welding. It Does Not.

Clothes coming from China are about three sizes smaller than the size on the tag says. I have lost count of the things I have ordered that don't show up at all.

I am a persistent person who does not like to give up, but I have been worn down by consistently writing and emailing and have had to write many things off.

Reassuring myself it was just a lesson – Who am I kidding!

When I was a teenager I would believe girls' stories, one careful owner "say no more" only to find out some had been around the block more times than the local taxi driver.

Some stories are written as I think of them, not in chronological order. One story often reminds me of another. Although I have written a few books I don't see myself as an author, just someone who likes telling stories.

When I was a teenager I had low self esteem, I wanted to be liked by the lads, who at that time had new, big motor bikes. I always felt inferior and for some unknown reason, a couple of the villains came around my house and I proudly showed them my dad's shed. My dad had lots of tools and all hung the walls in pristine condition.

Probably, coincidence but the next day my dad seemed puzzled as to why numerous tools were missing.

Another combination that does not go too well together is gullibility and drink. When Ian and Lisa were young we went to Majorca for a holiday.

To get a good deal we would all have to sleep in one room. Teresea, being the protector, would go to bed at the same time as the children. One night I just popped to the bar in the hotel for a night cap.

Not exactly sure what happened but I got friendly with this Spanish guy at the bar. I can remember getting on a coach with him and going somewhere. But I can't remember how much I paid for his antique leather jacket I came home with. I think I paid a little bit too much as he seemed to be friendly towards me for the remainder of our holiday.

One of my instructors and friend Stephen Jones often chuckles about the cameras' I bought from a passing salesman at my Dojo. The cameras were among the first small "movie" types. In fact, I left Stephen in my Dojo to go home to get the money to buy two.

The quality was brilliant, at least for the two minutes it lasted.

Martial Arts

A vast subject, so I'll again condense it to the area that I'm writing about. Easily taken in, when I started training karate, over fifty years ago I had never seen it before. Kicking was often used as a benchmark to portray one's ability, especially high kicking. I was never a natural athlete and also lacked flexibility. I had been involved in boxing prior to taking up karate; I was average, not a bad sparring partner but never championship material. Even though Mick Malt thought I was, thanks Mick but I like to be honest.

Back to high kicking, all the magazines portraying a karatika kicking high on the cover. To make matters worse, two of my fellow students who started at the same time as me, Alan White and Richard Gardiner, were both natural kickers.

In the Martial Arts magazines, stretching machines were being advertised. These showed before and after shots of what were obviously flexible people doing the splits after training with "The Flex master".

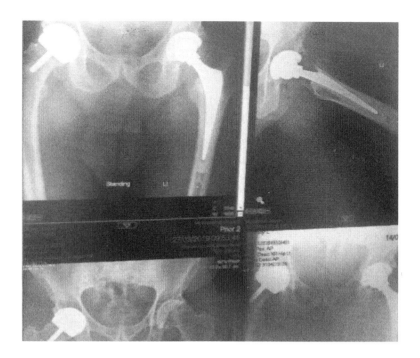

I think I bought the first one in this Country, along with every stretching aid.

I did eventually manage to kick to the head, for a short time, after having hypnotherapy, pulleys and Bob Lawrence's strong arms pushing my legs apart. I now have two hip replacements.

Kick Boxing Shows

I have hosted many kick boxing shows of different levels.

Putting on shows and making money, what a great combination. I started small, staging them at the Civic Hall in Grays.

I always put on entertainment shows, plenty of Razzmatazz, ring girls, demonstrations, dancers. I always gave good purses and trophies.

I even got my mum and dad involved. Mum made refreshments for the officials and dad was the timekeeper (He was an ABA Judge).

All my friends were involved in judging, Albie O'Connor, Mark Adams, Phil Jones and not forgetting the best MC in the Country Gary Hogben.

I bought over the American team several times, the Russians came over, the Welsh, Irish and Belgian.

Having made money on all the shows, Bob Lawrence who I was putting the shows with, and I thought we could stage a big one.

We staged our biggest show at the Brentwood Centre, we brought the Russian, American and British champions together. My own son Ian fought on the bill.

All the money we had made was put into this major event. Unfortunately we had not taken into consideration that at these, the crowd was mainly made up from the fighters own supporters. But we managed to half fill the Centre which would still have given us a profit, not what we expected but a small one.

Bob took a head count in the evening and worked out that even with our overheads we should still be ok.

After the success of the show no injuries, except for me nearly having an altercation with one loud member of the audience. I went home to count how much we had made. Five thousand pounds, not a profit but not a loss

How did that happen? Our fault, well perhaps mine, as Bob was, more sceptical as opposed to my trusting nature.

I think I may have overdone the razzmatazz a bit and got too prestigious trophies, but I had not taken into consideration the doorman could have been on the take, letting people in. Secondly the back door was conveniently left open and not all the trainers gave the right number of tickets sold, all of the profit on all the previous shows was lost.

I continued to stage shows at the Circus Tavern in Purfleet, making small profits but not enough to justify the time and stress it caused.

Motor Bikes

Recently when I moved to where I live, I got the inclination to buy a motorbike. So where do I look, "eBay".

Of course, it wasn't long until I bought my first one after not owning one for years. The problem was in the process of looking, which gave me an idea. If I was to bid on motor bikes that would be easy to sell, 125 cc was the most popular as that could be ridden with "L Plates", I could make money.

I also found someone who would collect them, what could go wrong!

I actually bought, had collected a couple and made a profit. That was until I got too ambitious.

I bought some new Chinese bikes at unbelievably low prices. I had ten motor bikes at that time. Great, all I had was to sell the three new Chinese bikes, still wrapped in plastic covering. These would be my profit.

The problem I had not taken into account was registering them.

Without the correct paperwork I could not sell them. Apparently it was common knowledge that Chinese motorbikes with no paperwork were useless as it was later

explained, they could have and probably were stolen or found on the beach with no VAT or Import Duty paid.

I did eventually sell them to owners of earlier models who probably changed the number plate to have a new old bike.

When I went out on the bike that I decided to keep, I didn't actually enjoy riding it. I think I lost my nerve a bit, so I came up with another idea. I saw that I could buy a Royal Enfield Combination, completely renovated from India. This sounds like a better option, three wheels as opposed to two. Having had combinations in the past and knowing how to handle them, I ordered one. I sold the solo I had; I did keep a vintage 1924 Peugeot and a Monkey Bike.

The Royal Enfield was a long time coming, but did eventually arrive. It was packed in a crate and it had to be lifted out by a forklift. Fortunately I live next door to a shed company who obliged.

When I excitedly went to see my combination which had been delivered, it was on its side. I think the company that delivered it did not have a big enough truck so put it on its side. When I opened the crate it was severely damaged. I managed to get it repaired, buying new parts including the tank and screen.

The bike ran and looked impressive, but unfortunately I had to go and have a new hip fitted which meant it would be difficult to start. Having only a kick-start, I was worried if it kicked back it would cause me problems.

I sold it at a reduced price and bought a Honda Goldwing. I had it transported from Newcastle, buying it on line with a new MOT and service. It was a stunner.

I loved riding it but had to go into hospital for my hip operation. So as to give it a run I let Tracy, one of my instructors use it.

When she brought it back, she said it probably needed a new battery as it was losing charge.

I found a mechanic who agreed to check the charging system, but said if it was an alternator it would be expensive. I showed him the receipts for a new alternator but he looked doubtful as there was no evidence of the engine being taken out.

However, he agreed to look at it. Jacqui and I dropped it off and set off to go fishing. After 5 mins he phoned to say come back to the workshop.

When I arrived he was looking upset, as he showed me the rotten parts that virtually held the frame together.

Unfortunately selling a vehicle knowing it was unsafe was not what I wanted to do.

I drove the bike gingerly home, being now aware of the condition. I put in an advert describing the condition, and fortunately sold it at a knock down price.

Cars

I know we all have bought "pups" over the years and don't feel sorry for myself at all, as a lot of mine was my own fault. Even the one with snow on it! Getting it home, when the snow melted only to find one wing was completely smashed! My fault, getting too excited to check, can't wait, I had a few cuts & shuts but it was the only way I could afford flashy cars.

However, I don't think I should be making the same mistakes at this time in my life!

When I went for my hip replacement consultation, my surgeon said I would not be able to drive for a couple of months. He saw my disappointment and suggested that I bought an automatic, preferably a 4 x 4 type; I could possibly reduce that to six weeks.

So..... my master plan, sell my Audi TT, which I felt confident would sell easily, look for a BMW as suggested.

As soon as you could say eBay, I borrowed some money and bought a well looked after, economical, BMW 5 x 5 auto, from a genuine man in Dagenham.

The Audi had not had too many callers, but I now had this not so economical BMW as I expected.

Meanwhile, my good friend Glenn asked if I was interested in his Porsche as it was immaculate and an Auto. Thinking I was able to sell the Audi and the BMW, I could buy it.

Problem one

I had difficulties in selling the BMW. I encountered various scams. Two different people offered to buy it without seeing it, paying by PayPal, only asking for a couple of hundred to be paid to the person collecting it, apparently a common scam.

Next a group of Eastern Europeans came, took for a test drive at about hundred miles an hour. Then discovered oil in the radiator, his accomplice, a supposed BMW mechanic, said it was the head gasket and would cost a fortune, offering scrap money.

I refused. Later finding out it was a common scam, the targeting of BMWs by Eastern Europeans, putting oil in the radiator. Not wanting to hold up Glenn on buying his new Porsches. I took the BMW to webuyanycar.com

They offered two thousand pounds on the phone, but reduced it to one thousand five hundred pounds when I took it to them.

I contacted another company who also bought cars for cash. The guy who came to look at it offered me two thousand pounds, a lot less than I paid.

I took it to his premises at Wickford, where his mechanic checked it over, then offered eighteen hundred pounds. I accepted as I was now in an embarrassing situation. As we were sorting out the paperwork. He checked on his computer, the details, to find out that it had been a right off prior to me buying it.

He reduced his offer to fifteen hundred pounds, which I accepted. I took the car to his premises and the mechanic was to drive me home, about twenty miles away.

Just before we reached my house, the car broke down, the engine light came on. The mechanic, who was probably part owner, gave me a choice, take it back or accept a thousand pound cash. I did, sometimes I have to ask myself about cash loss or stress.

Problem Two

As I had not sold the Audi and needed the cash, I asked a motor trader that I knew if he would put it on his forecourt and take a percentage of the sale. He agreed and being a convertible in the summer I assumed it would sell easily.

I naively thought that if I took the tax off and it was off the road I didn't need insurance. I was of course mistaken. I was threatened with prosecution. The dealer said he would help me by putting the car in his name, which wasn't a problem as he had the Log book and was selling it for me. Out of the blue I received a call from the dealer, he sounded distressed. "Jim, I have some bad news, the Receivers broke in last night and took the cars"-, if the car still had my name I could have protested and got my Audi back, but the rest is history.

Property

I am sure everyone has a story to tell about buying and selling their houses, and like having to look at holiday or baby photos can be awkward trying to seem interested. So I'll try to leave out the mundane bits and stick to what I'm writing about.

The first time I lost money on property was not being gullible but just bad timing. I had a property in Spain which gave me holidays, but when I was made redundant from Murco I had to sell. The unfortunate thing was that the weekend I went to complete the sale, the pound/peseta dropped the most in recent history, and if it had not been a Bank holiday in Spain it would have been alright.

The other problem was, when buying in Spain, you pay minimum tax but when selling the solicitors hold quite a lot of the money back supposedly for the government until they come to an "arrangement".

The money never got returned.

I have had properties in Brittany, Spain, Bulgaria and Egypt, I've lost on every one, but bad timing, and personal circumstances account for most. Selling Egypt, my Jewel in the Crown, was an adventure in itself.

Not using the property and having to pay maintenance every year forced me to sell at a greatly reduced price, which in itself hurt, paying £70,000 and selling it for under £20,000 was bad enough but the sale itself was a nightmare.

On the last day of my vacation with my friends John and Val, I had to complete the sale.

The buyers could not get to meet me until then, and it would have meant me going back. The day consisted of me being picked at six in the morning to drive to the city. As I had to leave the hotel with my luggage I had to visit my solicitors then the Police station then the Town Hall, passport office, and was eventually paid in Euros, Dollars, and Egyptian pounds. As I was leaving the solicitors he advised me I could not take Egyptian pounds out of the county, so had to find a dodgy money launderer in a side road to exchange at a low rate.

I just made it back to the Airport to meet my friends, carrying nearly £20,000 in cash.

When I got home I had to do something similar to change Dollars and Euros, again at a reduced rate as I had no proof of where it came from.

Bulgaria

Mark, one of my Black belts owned an Estate Agent, this is where I bought Egypt from but prior to that I bought a piece of land in Bulgaria, with the plan to build on. The proposition looked exciting and I shared the idea with a few friends.

I bought two plots, which were situated near to as we thought of a large town, Sunny Beach. When we all went over to see what we had bought, we were shocked to see how far it was from the town.

Admittedly, it was next to a large scenic Lake, but there was no infrastructure. In fact, it was near a poor village that had little in the way of facilities.

While we were there we were introduced to the builders who showed us pictures of the various houses that they were going to build near to the lake.

The builders 'Euro Build' were also building properties overlooking the Black Sea. They were offering a scheme of paying in instalments.

My friend Kam and I took up the offer; admittedly my one was in a prime location looking over the sea until a block of apartments were built -stopping my nice sea view. – Kam's was no better.

It turned out the builders were part of the Bulgarian Mafia!

I did have some nice holidays, but when I sold it, I got ripped off by the person I trusted to handle the sale, but there is nothing one can do, they are mostly crooked. I still think I own some land but cannot prove it, even if I could, taking someone to court is a waste of time.

My cousin Vic was investing in properties abroad and received a monthly magazine. He called me to tell me about the buy of the month, which was a buy-to-let in Bulgaria, the scheme was to invest in property in Bulgaria, with a guaranteed letting clause written in.

The idea was we paid £5,000 initially and then was, returned £3,000 (£2,000 for administration). The money would be put into a scheme where the Bulgarian Government would give a 100% loan and guarantee Lets, to pay the loan and profit.

I bought two of the flats, one for my daughter Lisa; Ian declined the offer, and many friends also bought in.

All was going well until we received an email. The email we received said the Bulgarian Government was no longer giving 100% mortgages and the money we paid in would be returned. So I was expecting £10,000 to be paid into my bank. This never happened and when tracing the number found it was a Call Centre.

We went to Scotland Yard who, although sympathetic ,said unfortunately this was small fry, even though it tallied up to nearly £100,000 altogether. Credit Card fraud was taking up all their resources.

I lost a couple of friends over this issue. I wonder if they thought I was a scammer.

As this book is not like my autobiography in as much as it's not in any form of Chronological order, some of my stories may seem confusing. It's because I think of things and something that sets off a similar series of events that I have forgotten.

When I meet an old friend or acquaintance they very often come out with a story I have forgotten, this is what prompted me to write *Ungifted*.

The idea behind writing *Ungifted* was to encourage people with no natural ability or low self-esteem that they can be successful.

I have done quite well in Martial Arts and other aspects of my life, which considering my lack of sporting or academic abilities is living proof, which I want to pass onto others in similar circumstances.

I was recently reading an article on significance, bringing to light the obvious by many, that we are all significant.

Comedians need audiences, as do musicians and all the gifted ones, but without us they would or could be insignificant.

I think of it as the honey bee and flower syndrome both need the other to survive.

Back to the Properties

One of my long term friends Mickey Griffin recently reminded me of one of our duel ventures.

Mick and I used to play squash on a Saturday -well it was more like full contact squash. One particular Saturday Mick had to go and visit his dad, who I knew well.

Jimmy Griffin, Entrepreneur and charismatic man with a good sense of humour was now living in a one room apartment, one of many in an old terraced house in Grays.

It was sad to see a successful, funny man who was also a brilliant sprayer in such a rundown place.

When Mick and I sat with him having a coffee, we both had the same thought bubble coming out of our heads.

No sooner had we thought about it, we acted. The idea was, we could buy a place, make it into flats and rent them out.

Mick is a very successful businessman who has worked extremely hard as a welder and property developer. He is very charismatic and talented, but does not suffer fools gladly. Mick has a fiery side to him which I will come to in the next part of this story.

I found a house which fitted our requirements, managed to borrow the money from the bank, my part of the project. Mick was to provide the practical side and could always lay his hand on "things".

The deal was finalised on a Friday, so we gave notice to the family and gave them an extra day to clear all of their furniture and possessions.

On Saturday, Mick and I turned up tools and material, only to find that no effort had been made to move out.

We politely asked the family to clear their stuff out and we would return later that day. We returned back in the afternoon only to find that the family was still there. To make matters worse the son, who was quite arrogant, was laying in his bed.

Both Mick and I were getting agitated and went up to the bedroom to have a stand-off with the son.

He said he would move his bits when he was good and ready. To say Mick saw red was an understatement. Mick went to his truck and returned with a sledge hammer, if the son thought it was an empty threat, he soon found out it was not.

Mick proceeded to knock the bedroom wall down, which was lath and plaster. Funny enough, the son, being covered with plaster, soon got up, cleared his bedroom and vacated the house.

We converted the house into two flats to either rent or sell. I have never worked so hard but it was worth it, so I thought.

No sooner had we finished the conversion which looked superb, (Mick is a perfectionist) I'm a bodger. The legislation changed regarding property in Thurrock. Flats required adequate parking space for four cars, and of course we had not allowed for that.

We spent the next weeks converting the flats back to one house

We did manage to sell, making a small profit. Mine went on buying a piano, as my children were learning to play. I still have the piano; it is the only piece of furniture I kept when we sold my family home when I split with Teresea. It has moved four times in different homes, but I still smile when I look at it.

When I was working at Murco, I was fortunate to enjoy a good lifestyle. I earned a good wage that allowed me to not only live in a large property, but buy a home in Spain, which I have spoken about. Because of the Buy to Let mortgages available, I bought a flat in East Tilbury.

What amazes me is that when you have money or high income the bank will try to lend whatever you want. But when you need it, you can't get it.

Over the years I have managed to buy a few flats in the same place -Stanford House.

I firstly must give a back drop on Stanford House to give a picture of the following stories.

East Tilbury was the location of the famous Shoe Factory -Bata, owned by Thomas Bata.

Working in the Bata Factory was one of the options that most school leavers had at the time. All the houses in East Tilbury up to the level crossing were owned by Bata: the Bata Estate, as it was known then, had its own swimming pool, shops and Social Club.

The employees would live in the houses; the management would live in the more prestigious ones.

A large hotel, Stanford House, was there for employers or visitors. When the factory closed down, the Hotel was sold to a large property developer.

The rooms were converted to Studios, one or two bedroom apartments. Investors would buy these and rent out to private tenants or ones on DSS as the purchase price was affordable to many of the public including me, they got snapped up as soon as they were on the market. Unfortunately, many were rented out to the DSS or people with low income. The clientele were not always the best. A great shame is that the hallway, foyer was very large, the apartment had scenic views but did seem to attract some less desirable tenants, as I will mention in the next part of this book.

Once again, I'll write in no specific order, as I also can't believe how many stories I have about just one subject.

Tenant No.1

A lovely, friendly couple came to my house wanting to rent one of my flats. They told me that they wanted to have the property for an indefinite time; I showed them the property which they loved. We agreed on a rent; in fact I reduced it as they seemed so genuine. They agreed to bring the cash around my house every Friday; fine again, very pleasant and paid the full amount. The next Friday the man came on his own, pitifully telling me he had not much work that week and could only afford to pay part of the rent. I accepted but was suspicious as he smelt of alcohol.

This situation happened the following week, he looked a bit drunk or stoned.

A few weeks went by without payment, when I managed to contact his girlfriend, she came up with a cock and bull story, he had left her as she was pregnant.

I went to give them an unannounced visit, I knocked on the door, and I heard voices, so I knew they were in. I never know if on these occasions, I feel fear or adrenalin when approaching the property.

The man opened the door; he was surprised to see me, came out and started shouting at me, threatening to break my knee caps. I snapped, fear, adrenalin I don't know, but he ran backwards into the apartment quicker than I could go forward. They eventually moved out, leaving the place in a state, owing me money.

Tenant No 2.

This time the tenant was smart, big and black. He paid a couple of months rent up front, but again stopped and would not reply to my messages, so once again I had to go and visit him, being not big or intimidating looking, puts me at a disadvantage. Albie insisted I took a weapon with me, which I did. Again, not sure if climbing the stairs, adrenaline or fear made my heart beat faster.

I gingerly knocked at the door partly hoping he was out partly hoping he was in. When there was no reply I opened the door and tried to get in. The door was jammed, my heart was beating, the reason that the door was stuck was the pile of letters.

The apartment was empty, only piles of letters. All of the letters contained Bills, Credit Cards and Statements. Yes of course it was only an address that had enabled my tenant to obtain cards, loans and anything on Tick.

Tenant No.3

I must say that not all of my tenants have been crooked, a couple were fine, strangely enough I knew them.

Once again, I went on my dreaded visit to try to get my rent arrears. The person this time was not too bad, or what I thought, I sat down and spoke to him. He agreed to pay when his giro came in; I had to accept his offer but told him I would "be back."

I received a letter from him, which I still have, it was a long well written letter accusing me of having him beaten up! In fact he said two men came in and inflicted serious damages on him while he was in bed, and next time I went down there to see him, he would have a shotgun waiting for me. I took the letter to the police, whose answer was we can't do anything as it is just a threat!

Before I could go down and re visit him, I had a call from the caretaker asking me to come to the apartment as soon as I could. What had happened was the tenant had moved out, but took the immersion heater with him, (copper) .If this was not bad in itself, and it had not only flooded my apartment, but the Post Office below. No rent, No immersion heater and the damage it had caused. I tried to track him down to no avail.

Tenant No.4

For the first years of letting my apartments to a Nigerian Nurse, I had no trouble; in fact I thought she was the perfect tenant. When she was late paying her rent she would let me know and catch up when she could. In fairness she did not complain or ask for much.

One day she contacted me regarding a window problem. Dave Perry, one of my instructors, is a good handyman. He went to assess the problem for me. He managed to sort out the problem, but did tell me about the state of the place.

This, I must take on board as my mistake, I should have gone and inspected the place, but I did what I sometimes do, is bury my head in the sand.

This was not until the caretaker phoned to tell me she had moved out, taking lots of boxes with her. He told me he got a glimpse of the state of the place.

I went down to check the place out, I arranged for a handyman to break in, as I had not a recent key. When I arrived the handyman was in, he told me to be prepared for a shock. I cannot describe the state of the place, (see photo).

I wish I had more literacy skills or vocabulary to give an adequate description of the state of the place. I now decided to sell it. Another story.

The handyman and his son worked extremely hard trying to clear out the debris. Whilst packing bits his son found several phones and Televisions. I said he could have them, as he was helping.

That evening the dad phoned me, he said they had found child pornography on the phone and suggested I take it to the Police station. I did but I was disappointed again that they didn't do anything about it.

I cleared the remaining bits and dumped them behind the Dojo where I train.

The lady returned to the flat and said she had not moved out and wanted her bits. Several texts and phone calls later she threatened to send her brother and his entourage to sort me out.

Fortunately for me the time she told me they were on their way, I was in my Dojo with not only a class of students but enough weapons to arm a group of Samurai.

I eventually redecorated, fitted a new kitchen and carpet and sold it.

Tenant No.5

This time I rented through an Agency Bairstow Eves or Bastard thieves as they are effectively known. I made the mistake of not reading the small print perhaps because I could not find a strong enough magnifying glass. I believed that the Agents were to inspect the property and report any damage or irregularities – Big Mistake!

The tenant paid six months rent up front, so for six months I didn't worry. After that the rent came in, but late or in parts. I did not get concerned as I wrongly

assumed the Agents were responsible. What did concern me was when the caretaker phoned to tell me the tenant was caught on CCTV taking two GOATS into the apartment.

I contacted the Agents; they did phone the tenant to get them removed. A first floor apartment in which pets are not allowed was not what I was paying for. In fact when the tenants moved out he owed me £1500 and cost me another £500 to remove his rubbish, also I had to replace the bathroom and carpets. I took the Agents to the Ombudsman and managed to get £200 back from the money I had been paying them, their excuse for not inspecting the property as agreed was "the tenant was never in".

This was the last straw, I was going to refurbish and sell. Easier said than done.

The Management Company that I paid every six months to plus an exorbitant amount of insurance, was called CBS Estates.

When you sell an apartment, they have to supply various information to allow the sale to go ahead, this encounters cost, but just wanting to sell the property was the least of my concerns. But the company was crooked. They delay giving the information which often results in the sale falling through.

This happened with two apartments I owned in fact I lost six buyers in all. As well as the stress it caused it forced me into taking out loans as I was no longer receiving rental income, but I still had to pay the mortgages, on top of that was solicitor's fees for the non sales. I accept the legitimate fees had to be paid plus the

Estate Agency fees but to ensure I sold the properties I also had to greatly reduce the price.

I suspected something was not "Kosher" not just because the owners and management were Jewish but because the CDS Management kept phoning me offering to buy the property at a silly price. I have found out that this has been done to several other owners and have subsequently lost their sale.

I have been in contact with the Trading Standards who are now investigating.

My experience with Sam from CDS was very stressful as I would phone every day as did my solicitors. He either hung up or made excuses. I was prepared to go to their London Office but even the address seemed false.

Selling and paying back money I owed was one of the most stressful times of my life.

Jacqui, who I had met 3 years before, assisted in clearing out the properties and cleaning for me, as she wrote in the introduction of this book was now witness to some of my ventures or adventures.

Another property story was when I downsized to a Mobile Home near Battlesbridge. Life seemed simple, I bought a luxury Park Home, something I would never have envisaged doing, but when I took my daughter to Maldon to look at a house she was to rent, we stopped and looked at Hayes Farm Park, as she had seen how nice the homes were.

While walking around the park we spoke to a lady who had a home looking over the fields, coincidence or karma I don't know but she said she was selling her home.

She showed us her immaculate place.

At the time I had no intention of selling my Bungalow in a small village in Bulphan. But seeing the view and the inside of the home started me thinking. If I sold Bulphan and one of my properties, paid back the mortgage, and took out a small loan, I could buy this place with cash, no mortgage for the first time in my life.

I told the lady, Pauline, I would think about it and give her an answer the next day.

Lisa, George and I were due to go to Bulgaria that weekend. Yes ,you guessed! I agreed to the price and left a deposit on our way to the Airport.

On our journey to the Airport we had to divert to pay Lisa's rent, so it did not give us a lot of time, only more stress – we discovered I had the wrong tickets for the flight – Lisa phoned the holiday company and managed to get a replacement which we picked up at the airport.

At the time I still owned a property in Bulgaria, but as it had a balcony, low rails I thought it was too dangerous as George was only two years old, so I contacted the man who looked after mine to see if he had a more suitable place, he said he had one in a nearby town.

Arriving at three in the morning tired with a two year old, being dropped off by the taxi, we could not wait to get in our apartment.

We climbed the stairs, suitcases and George only to find out the key was not in the place it should have been.

I tried phoning Steve the supposed owner but got no reply. There was no one in the security office.

I eventually managed to find someone to explain our predicament, who kindly found a room for the night.

I managed to contact Steve who came, sheepishly and a bit suspiciously, he did get us a room but not the one we have been told we were having.

Looking back, I think he sub let one of the properties he was looking after, and I am sure he did to mine in the winter. I also think he made a bit more on my place when I trusted him to sort out the sale.

Back home I eventually sold my Bungalow in Bulphan and bought the Park Home.

I loved it there, all the new furniture, Jacuzzi Bath and a view to die for.

When I came home one evening there was a letter waiting for me. It was a notification that new homes were to be sited in front of ours. It was anonymous but everyone thought it was one of the residents.

Fred Sine was a ruthless multi billionaire who came from a traveller background. He was the owner of the site and many more and a bully who everyone on the site feared. He had beaten up people on numerous occasions and kicked down fences – he did what he liked. He was squeezing more homes in by the day so it was feasible he would buy the farmers land to build in the green belt land to build new homes on.

I panicked; I did not want to be a few feet away from other places that would block my view. I put my home on the market and it sold the next day. I did not tell the estate agents about the possibility of the homes being put in front of mine.

I was a bit lucky regarding Fred as his JCB driver Clinton, a tough man, was good friends with a friend of mine, Andy Courtney. For once in my life I did not mind a bit of exaggeration regarding my skills or reputation, the stories filtered back to Fred and his bodyguard, so I was left alone.

I could not afford to buy anything as I had to pay 10 per cent to the site when I sold my home, and due to wealth and age, I could not get a mortgage.

I heard that the place I now live in was to become vacant, although the rent was more than I could really afford, it fit the bill with a large garden, a large detached Bungalow out of the way.

I came up with a plan to put the money I got from my sold home into putting deposits into three flats to buy to let with the profit to pay my rent. This worked for a while until COVID where this stopped my income and one of the tenants stopped paying the rent. To add insult to injury another situation then occurred.

I bought two of the flats from my badminton coach Alison, who had some personal problems. Both had tenants, She took me to the tenants and introduced me to them and assured them they would be looked after by me. One of the properties was not in the best of conditions – the tenant appeared a little rough and edgy. I have had to get a fair few jobs done but in all fairness he has been no trouble, touch wood!

The other tenant was the other extreme: a gay man who

had the place filled up with antiques, paintings and looked immaculate. My thinking was that if he ran away or stopped paying the rent, I could sell the antiques and retire.

David was no trouble but was not in good health. I sadly got notification that the payments had stopped due to him passing away. David's sister-in-law went to the flat to sort out his affairs telling me she had come down from Newcastle, she said her family had not been able to leave it as clean as they would have hoped due to a short stay but all that was needed was a light dusting.

Jacqui and I arrived at the flat and nearly fainted: the family had ransacked the flat, leaving more junk and rubbish than I had ever seen. Two skips full of rubbish and weeks of cleaning before I could even consider re renting it out.

I found out the nice polite man I rented to had a tainted sexual past resulting in an ASBO and was hated by all of the neighbours – once again my judgement was not as sound as I had hoped!

As well as the flats I had bought to subsidise my rent, I had also bought a one bedroom house in Woodham Ferrers with a sitting tenant. When I did not receive the rent I decided to go and knock to introduce myself. I knocked on the door and was less than pleased to have to ask about the rent but the man was a reasonable person and it transpired that the estate agent had not bothered to advise the tenant about the change in payment. His rent was still going to the previous owner. Bairstow Eves took no responsibility for their mistake.

The tenant moved out and the new one moved in, the original ones had decorated it to a top standard and left it in the same condition.

The new tenants asked for the stair carpet to be repaired which I obliged with as I wanted good tenants. For a year they were no trouble until they had problems with their payments and eventually stopped paying completely. They did not answer any correspondence from me or the Estate agents. I agreed during the lockdown that they could pay half the rent, I had hoped for some loyalty and respect.

I had been suffering with a painful hip and decided to go for a replacement. The healing process took longer than I had anticipated and I contracted Bursitis. This is painful and some days I have problems with walking but others I am like Bruce Lee! Gradually, after getting my life back after this hip replacement and the first lockdown, I wanted some normality.

I decided to take my Boat out for a run on the Crouch. Lisa, Chris, George and Esme joined me on a sunny afternoon. When taking the Boat on the Crouch, you have to allow for the tides. The tide changes come in and out quickly and can be dangerous. I normally allow for at least an hour before high tide to come back in, so I had planned to stay out for a couple of hours then confidentially get back. It was a lovely Sunny day. Chris had said he was thinking of getting rid of his Kayak and getting a bigger one so they could all go out so I suggested he use the boat

when he wanted to. He accepted this offer and said he would take the wheel. I sat back and relaxed with a beer when I heard and felt a thud and thought he had hit something. He thought he had grounded it. We realised the steering had failed. Now we had no steering and at least an hour up the Crouch and the tide started to change. We were drifting towards the expensive Yachts and luxury boats. I kept trying to start the engine and was going round in circles.

Eventually a boat saw us in distress, as was Lisa, and they towed us to a mooring nearby that was luckily next to Chris stepdad's so we were able to walk back to Lisa's house, then return to the car.

As if that incident was not enough, when we checked the mooring and we saw it had collapsed – whether or not it was when my boat came away and it had been holding it up and then collapsed or it had been hit, we will never know.

As we were near to Woodman, I decided to pay my tenant a visit. I had never met him but knew he was a builder. I limped to the door and a tattooed Jack the Lad opened the door, I said

'I am your landlord and I want my rent'

Funny really as I was limping, the wrong side of sixty and not intimidating where he looked aggressive and even took off his coat, I jumped into the front room like a Gazelle.

I don't know why but he decided to back down. I got a text at 6 am the next morning saying he did not want any stress and the money would be paid on Thursday, which it was. The Estate agent then called and said if I went round again the Police would be called. He has since moved out and when I went to inspect I was shocked to see how clean and tidy it had been left. Unfortunately the new Tenants are Mr. and Mrs. Pedantic and I am currently working through their never ending list of demands.

Car Sales

When I mentioned to one of my students that I was selling my car, he offered his front garden as a forecourt. As I had already put my Audi in my forecourt I thought it would be a good idea if I purchased another. Lee was not working so we said we split the profit.

Good old eBay! I found a bargain low mileage car VW Beetle – the problem was it was in Leicester. No problem, a day out for Jacqui and me. I booked the train tickets and we were on our way – well, not exactly. At Paddington we had to rush to get the train – out of character I was cutting it fine... We made it and was just relaxing and ordering a coffee when the ticket inspector advised we were on the wrong train!

The Painful Side of Being Gullible

In my late teens, I became friends with Peter Lalley, who I shared numerous adventures with. As our friendship grew, so did our group of friends. Peter had a cousin, who had a caravan in Great Yarmouth which a group of us rented. They all had good jobs and went dressed in their designer clothes; I had my Mr. Byrite copy ones.

Whilst in Yarmouth, having great fun we had lunchtime drinks as part of our lunchtime routine. One lunchtime whilst having drinks, I was drinking halves to the others pints as I was not a great drinker. They would say I would get drunk on a wine gum or the Barmaids apron!

This particular lunchtime was different. A girl came up to us with a brown paper bag and asked if anyone wanted to buy a jumper. Never wanting to miss an opportunity I jumped at the idea saying I would buy it before even asking the price! To say I looked smug was an under-statement showing off my bargain jumper to the lads. This was when a lad built like Mike Tyson wearing a crew neck jumper came over swearing, demanding to know why I was holding his jumper. My voice sounded high pitched when I stood up to him. We went outside the pub to settle this misunderstanding and before I had a chance to explain or give him a McAllister hook, he hit me with the hardest punch I had ever received and I have had a few in my lifetime! It landed on my left ear and I saw stars, so my attempt to hit back was pathetic. He was right to hit me as I was wearing his jumper, I explained what had happened and we went in for a drink together.

As we were walking up the high street, I saw the girl in the Fish and chip shop who had sold me the jumper, buying fish and chips for her friends with my ten bob! With a throbbing ear I jumped into the shop and grabbed her handbag but she screamed and the shop Assistant threatened to call the police so I had to return it!

Recently I bumped into one of the boys at the local golf club and he relayed the story to the people I was with, ironically the owner was telling a group of people how I had beat up a group of gipsies which never happened. I left before they did, but it was a good story for my ego.

Boot Sales

Going to a boot sale, I am like a diabetic going to a sweet shop! Too much choice and I never come back empty handed. My Dad, as gullible as me, used to go every Sunday and sneak bits into the shed so my Mum would not see what he bought. He would give most of what he bought away, but liked the thrill of buying things, which me and my Daughter can relate to.

I have had some bargains but also dodgy electrical things!

Neil Cooper, one of my students and friends, helps me out and is a computer and electrical whiz kid that came up with a way I could make some money.

He proposed an idea that whenever I was planning on buying something I should phone him first and then give him half of the money I saved – he was joking but I nearly took him up on this idea!

When I look back on my life, I chuckle on my adventures. Even when buying a glass set in Spain against all the warnings. When I opened it at home to find none of the glass matched and what did was broken!

Mark Adams, a shrewd very talented Martial Artist, had called to see how I was. He was one of the consortium who bought into the buy to let scheme – he put on facebook a photo of a leather flying jacket, a fake one he received but he still looked good in it. I wonder if gullibility can be transmitted.

Peter Lalley, as I mentioned earlier, had a gift of painting Technicolor pictures out of black and white photos. Not literally – he was able to embellish and for my hunger to believe it's no wonder I ended up in situations I might otherwise have avoided.

I worked in an office in London, quite cushty starting at 9:30 and finishing at 5:30. My job was to deliver mail, help with office jobs and learn about shipping to eventually become a broker.

Peter convinced me that working with him in Magnet Timber would be much better. Getting home early, being able to wear jeans, lots of girls, more money, but although London was not a bad job, after waiting for the train I wasn't getting home until after seven each night. To my Dads disappointment, I handed in my notice to go and work as a Door lift man starting at 730 each morning. Lifting doors was hard work and I felt like I had done a day's work by the time I would have started at 930. As for the girls, to steal a phrase from my friend Geoff Thomson, one had a face like a blind cobbler's thumb, another looked like a robber's dog, I lasted three months.

At School, I was no angel, naughty rather than bad.

I got caught for many things of causing mischief and for being a clown and was often given the slipper. I also remember taking the slipper when I was framed for other classmate's actions. I had the Cane, the slipper, the leg of the chair and many other objects.

Once a classmate said, next time you get the cane Jimmy which was not a good name Jimmy McAllister for a boy with a stutter, put orange peel on your hands – I almost couldn't wait to get caned to try this out, smiling inside I rubbed the magic lotion on my hand and held them out for six of the best. I think I actually cried with the pain and the added bonus of citrus in the wounds.

Yarmouth

After my last trip to Yarmouth and bringing back a thick ear as a memento, I should have kept away!

My Karate classes and I used to have a yearly day trip to Margate (Beano).

The tradition was to call in a Beano pub on the way and call back again on the way back. The Roman Galley was the most popular one and also featured on Only Fools and Horses. In the first year we witnessed more fights here than any other pub.

As Martial Artists, it is sometimes difficult to stay out of fights; we work hard but play hard.

I came up with an idea that might keep us out of trouble but at the same time to get us into more pubs without being turned away. This idea was one of my better ones. Every year we should have a theme, we dressed as Vicars and Nurses, boys from up North, Morris Dancers and more others than I can remember. Having a few characters in our group helped, when the theme was blind people and one walked into the female toilets in the M2 cafe.

We performed a martial Art type dance as Morris

dancers on the Beach. There was never any trouble and the other Beano groups got to know us although some would actually believe we were who we were dressed as.

When we planned our trip, we decided one year that we would try a different resort – Yarmouth. I opposed it as I did not want to spend all day travelling in a mini bus but I was outvoted. To console me of my whining, the lads told me we were going to travel in style. The mini bus was American style with comfortable seats, a bar and all the latest mod comes.

I agreed, in fact the way they described it, I wanted to be picked up first instead of last to impress my neighbours.

When the bus arrived, instead of it being like the A Team bus, it was a rough looking bus with a toot like the sound of a Christmas cracker.

To make things worse, I had to sit on the engine cover. There was no pecking order here. I was one of the boys and that never changed and I would not have wanted it to. In fact, in my Thursday class, I still make the sandwiches.

To make things worse the bus broke down on the Yarmouth Bridge.

Another incident with us being the Blind group was at the services. One of the lads was playing a one armed bandit. A person watching asked how he knew what was going on, one of our quick witted gang said

'he can feel the vibration'

'Oh I see' said the spectator.

When we were as Vicars, Mick Griffin was dressed as

the Pope, and really got in on the act by dropping to his knees and kissing the floor in the pub. Half the pub looked shocked and half amazed!

Mickey Griffin

I have mentioned Mickey before and he is a good friend. He talked me into entering for the prison break charity race where the idea was to raise money for Chelmsford prison. The idea was to dress as convicts and select a category to find a way to get the furthest away from the prison in eight hours. As I had completed the London to Brighton ride a few times, Mick suggested that I enter. I thought it would be a ride in the park. Six of us were taken to Chelmsford Prison in Mick's van. The van would be our support vehicle carrying all of our personal possessions and our going out clothes. Mick had a caravan in Yarmouth and the idea was to ride to Yarmouth, stay the night and go to the clubs without worrying about drink driving. The A12 is slightly longer on a bike.

All was fine until we got to Ipswich Bridge, my cousin John and I got separated from the others which caused a

problem – this was before mobile phones. We had no money to get drinks with and we could not find our caravan park as we discovered there are many in Yarmouth! As I mentioned, I had completed the London to Brighton a few times never getting off my bike, only to stop for a drink. I prided myself on riding up the Deachley Deacon steep hill every year after a few drinks. The London to Brighton route is about sixty five miles and Chelmsford to Yarmouth is about 80 miles, which did not seem bad in principle. We were the only ones with no support, no van, and money. We went into the pub and explained what had happened and were lucky as they gave us light refreshments.

Now, slightly concerned we soldiered on, the next miles getting harder and harder. Ten miles from Yarmouth my legs turned to jelly. The most amazing thing then happened, five miles from Yarmouth we heard a shout. Mick had recognised me from the way I rode, we arrived at the caravan and I slumped into a chair. I struggled to walk to the pub where I managed food, one beer and crashed out.

The highlight was that we won the category and out of all my trophies this had been the hardest one I got. In fact we rode 100 miles.

Catching up with an old friend who is featured in this book, Terry Griffiths, was nice as we hadn't been in touch much over the last couple of years. The common theme when talking to friends is that they remember something different about me and Terry reminded me of when I was teaching a student at my dojo who told me he was building a kit car. I had never heard of a kit car but it intrigued me. The concept is that you buy a donor car and have it fitted with a shell over it. When completed it looks like a replica of various designs. Of course I did not have the patience or ability, but I wanted to have another interest as well as Martial Arts.

I located a JVR not far away that looked like a Morgan or MG; in fact I got into car shows with it and used to take my Dad with me. We got really close during these days out together. He would reminisce about his old cars and tell me stories about him and his friends driving experiences. My dad drove a lorry and a landing craft in the war and he would tell me the same stories at every car show we went to. I know I now do the same, we turn into our parents!

At one show in Dichley in Kent, I saw my dream car. A green Royale Sabre and immediately fell in love with it.

Talking to the owner, Ken Baker, he said he would sell it if he got the right price. I promised I would contact him on Monday after going to the bank, but I ended up giving him a deposit on the same day, good old Dad! I use this car all the time and love it more now than when I got it. I could make more money if I sold it out than I paid but I love it and it is a real head turner.

Only one problem with this venture, I had to sell my JVR to pay for it. It did not have many miles on the clock as was only used for special occasions. I felt confident I would get my money back for it, had the paintwork touched up by my friend Geoff and the engine was perfect. I got a call from a gentleman who said he wanted to buy an English classic replica and have it shipped to Germany.

I cleaned it and started the car, proud to show it to the German man coming to see it and was hoping he would pay and take it with him. As anyone knows, selling anything can be stressful; I can never hide how much I want to buy something and can never play poker.

John Mcfahn, a friend I used to work with, said if I won the lottery you would see the money burning a hole in my pocket.

Back to the car. Two German men arrived with a lady. She was dressed like a go go dancer, micro leather skirt, not that I noticed!

The two men were looking over the car with me watching their reactions. I'm nobody's fool, the lady asked to use my bathroom – as I lived on my own with no one in the house, I showed her where it was. I waited in the hall for what seemed like hours. I did not want to seem like a pervert but did not like the idea of someone I didn't know being alone in my house – I've been robbed three times by possibly a cleaner or someone who had access to my house. When she eventually came out, we went to the bottom of the garden where the car was in my garage. The men asked to take the car for a spin. I started it up and it took a few attempts which was unusual and eventually started. I thought it may be due to me not using it much but it had run fine earlier. It drove like a kangaroo, I was annoyed and embarrassed. When I got back my intention was to phone my friend Geoff but the strange thing was they still seemed interested in the car. They had a private discussion and said they had a car and trailer ready so would take it at a knocked down price, any other time I may have agreed but something felt wrong so I refused. They demanded I did and got aggressive. This was probably the best thing they could have done. My friends say people see my politeness as a weakness. I was annoyed with what had happened, and with their attitude, I saw red. Pay the amount I asked or clear off or words to that effect were used. When I told my friends what had happened they said it was an old trick buyers used with the lady distracting me whilst they tampered with the car pulling the plug leads out to malfunction the engine. There was no car or trailer. But they did buy the car, close shave this time!

Bargain video

When video recorders first came out on the market, there were two formats: V.H.S or Betamax. The technical friends that I had, said that Betamax was the better quality but V.H.S was the more popular one in the video retail shops. Second hand goods were normally advertised in the local paper or exchange and Mart. Of course I wanted one. My Dad, being an older version of me, found one in the Exchange and Mart. Unfortunately it was in Braintree some fifty miles away. The distance did not really bother us and was seen as a day out and I had travelled round the country to buy a car or two! The other thing we had to consider was the format. It was a Grundig. My Dad had Grundig tape recorder and was told by his workmates that this was the best electronic device on the market! Being German this was better than the Japanese version. He was right, the German technology was known for being superior to any other counties, the only problem was that there were two types. My work colleague Fred Addams, a Techno buff, endorsed how good this was.

Dad and I went to Braintree, dark and rainy and it took us hours to find the house, two excited buyaholics is not a good combination! We found the house, nice street, nice people and they convinced us that this was the best system showing us films they had recorded. The quality was perfect. It was embarrassing when one of the films they showed us was 'blue'. My Dad, an ex marine and Docker got embarrassed by this. Nevertheless we bought the recorder.

All was fine, it worked well but I could not get any videos from the rental shop although it recorded fine. The only other problem was that it was impossible to buy the large video cassettes to record on which were not unlike the ones I had in my car.

My friend Tony could get hold of anything, he was the one who had got hold of the clocks and drills. His cousin John was the one who actively obtained the bits, where and how I never asked.

On my Son Ian's Birthday, we were going to London to Madame Tussauds and Planet Hollywood for his Birthday treat. As we were leaving, I got a phone call from John asking if he could stash a couple of goody bags in my garage as he was being observed by the Police. I agreed, but Teresea overheard this conversation which led to an argument that created tension on the drive to London and I felt guilty for my poor children as the day was a disaster. I also had to keep stopping to put water into the car and got stuck in heavy traffic whilst wondering what John had put in the garage.

As soon as we got home I went to investigate the bags in the garage. I could not open the door so had to use the side door. The garage was jam packed with black sacks, an engine and speed boat! The atmosphere was not great but I managed to offload the black sacks, the engine and the speed boat, to various friends.

One other thing I had bought off John was an electronic device that stopped the electric metre working in the form of a black metal box.

This was used for a couple of weeks which was great – free electric – until I got a visit from the Police. The metre had abrasions around the wires and was reported by the metre reader and it was suspected I had tampered with the wiring. If I came clean I could be charged with theft. Of course I was furious at their accusations, I was a Fire officer of an oil company – I explained the wiring had come loose due to the subsistence of the house and was able to prove it by showing the officers the dropping of the path. As soon as they left I destroyed the box.

The Beatles

I love the Beatles, always have and am lucky enough to have seen them live twice. Once in Southend and again in Finsbury Park in London. They were supported by Cilla Black, Gerry and the Pacemakers and Rolf Harris!

At School most of my clothes were second hand as my parents could not afford the Italian suits or trousers with Tapered legs. In my last year of School the Beatles were just becoming famous. I let my hair grow forward into a fringe. Only once did I defy my Mum and the eighteen inch trousers became known as bell bottoms – I took them to Mrs. Bower to get them tapered, but it went wrong and she only tapered the bottom part which made them look like jodhpurs – not having Winklepicker shoes to go with them I only had sensible School shoes which made them look worse.

This was to change. The Beatles were not only a new genre of music but set off a whole new fashion, hair, Beatles boots and jackets with no collar. I wanted one but could not afford one – good old Mum she was good at making things and I had won many fancy dress competitions with her skills.

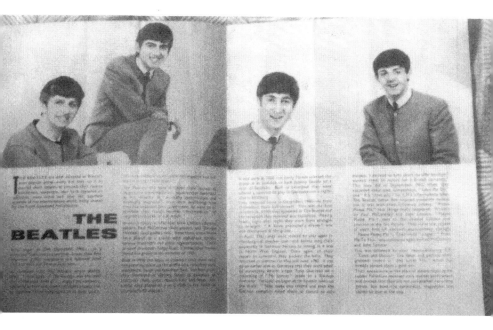

Mum cut off the collar on my School jacket, sewed it and made it into a Beatle jacket – one problem she had not thought of was that the coat had no collar and no matter how many times it was pressed the lapel would still have the same crease in and return to its original shape, so now I only had one school jacket – not a Beatles jacket but just an ordinary one with no collar!

School uniforms were not compulsory only for School trips so I had to wear a weird jacket for the rest of my school days.

Boxing Gloves

Without wanting to sound conceited, I know a lot of people – this is not a bad thing but I also have a bad memory for names and faces.

When I meet someone, I don't remember them and have to ask a set of questions to give me a clue:

What are you up to?'

'Do you still work at the same place?'

I can remember stories about people but can't remember who was involved. One of my students, who regularly trained at my house (I had a boxing ring and gym in the garden), was always coming up with 'bits' that according to him were legit. He had a business collecting rubbish and a lot were only slightly marked or damaged. He told me he had a large amount of boxing equipment coming and would be interested. Is the Pope Catholic?! He dropped off hundreds of boxes with focus mitts and boxing gloves that were good enough to sell on. As a bonus he threw in loads of speed balls, floor to ceiling balls and punch bags. I could not lose.

I was to sell to students at a low price where I was to make money. There was only one small problem. When laying out the gloves I noticed something was not quite right.

Most of the gloves were left-handed – the speed balls and floor to ceiling balls would not stay up. I can't remember if my student ever came back.

Chain Letters

As a child I would send chain letters to people – I would send five and wait patiently for a hundred to come back. I think I might have received one back.

The best salesmen are the ones who do not do any actual selling – I found this out. Teresea's friend Trish, who was also my next door neighbour as a child in Stifford Clays, brought her new Husband Alan to meet us. Alan was a charming man and I liked him from the off. He had been made redundant from a building company having been a director. I am always intrigued by what people do for a living. Knowing Alan had recently lost his job, I trod carefully at first but it was apparent he had no money problems. I felt comfortable asking how he was managing without a job.

He dismissed my question in a polite way, but left the door open for me to push a bit. Alan hinted that he had money making ventures; he also said he had past bad experiences when friends had become involved and did not want to do it again. They say that curiosity killed the Cat – my symbol in Karate is a Lion that says it all!

Over the course of the evening, Alan gave me bit by bit

bait sized information and said every day he received money. The principle was not dissimilar to chain letters and if I were to enrol ten people to cover the initial joining up fee, I would receive a regular income if I enrolled people. I did manage to get twenty people on board as although I was known for being a soft touch I was also known for being honest.

I would never knowingly catch someone even if I did not know them – apart from the Electric board! This scheme did no more than get the money back I paid in but I saw my friends lose money.

I am currently watching a series called My Name is Earl – an American series where he has a list of everyone he has done wrong to and how he has this KARMA – I have all the people who were misled on mine.

Bull Worker

Buying chest expanders and a bull worker in my teens, was not wrong or a mistake the only mistake I made was not using them. Would I change my life – No!

I was recommended by world Athlete Fatima Whitbread, who I knew, and had a brother in my Kickboxing class, to be involved in a Martial Arts competition in Cyprus.

I felt honoured and excited, so much that without asking enough questions, I accepted. I have selective reading in that, my eyes skip the parts I do not want to read and pick out the good bits, which sum it up for me. When reading an insurance policy I read the parts I want to see.

I read I was going to get paid for judging and refereeing, but I did not realise that this was only for the days I would be required. And had to pay for my flights and hotel. I was only required for five days out of the seven and to add insult to injury the hotel was basic with no food supplied during the day. I suspect this was a criminal event, as I saw a lot of smartly dressed gentlemen exchanging money. I consoled myself by savouring the

experience. There was a problem with paying the bill on my last day – I had not prepared to pay for the hotel or the coach to the hotel and only had limited cash on me.

When I went to pay for the hotel with my credit card, they said they would only accept cash. As I said basic I now wondered if the hotel owners knew we were using the hotel as it was closed season. The pleasant receptionist was replaced by a sleazy looking Cyprian in a Mafia Suit who told me he had a solution and I should go with him. At this time I wondered if the concrete overcoat did exist!

I went with him in his car for what seemed like hours driving through towns and villages until we came to another Town. I did not know where we were, but followed instructions to follow him, trying to not show my fear or anguish. We eventually reached our destination –a travel agent. What I had to do was book a nonexistent holiday that came to the amount of my hotel bill. Getting back to the hotel was the most relief I had experienced in my life and the overpriced beer was worth it!

One of the strange things in writing this book is the soul searching aspect – I think everyone should write a book about their lives. It can help others not to make the mistakes that they have and to give good honest tips about experiences they have had and benefited from.

I was telling my friend Don last week about this book. Don has known me for some time and witnessed money misadventures around me. He asked if I would change my life and the answer was, not at all.

I do see the best in people and want to trust and not be caught, but as this book shows my world is different to that.

I did not realise that Jimmy Saville was what we know now about him, I just thought that he was an eccentric do-gooder.

Ian, my son, is naturally cynical, takes his time to make decisions and does not suffer fools. In fact he bought me a book called *Mail-order Mysteries* about advertising and newspaper articles and many of the subjects in this book. But Ian did tell me of the time he helped his friend carry a large heavy container which supposedly contained a TV, up flights of stairs to find out it was a box of bricks!

I think someone secretly fitted a microchip inside my head when I was asleep that makes my head turn when I go past a for sale sign!

One downside to being too trusting is that it opens the door to opportunists.

I have been robbed a few times.

I have had cash stolen from my house and apart from the downside of losing money it has been made worse as it had to be from people I knew.

I won't name names but unfortunately when you have suspects you suspect all people who have access to your house and I spent a holiday once thinking whom it may be.

I have also had swords stolen from my gym in my house. What was also disturbing was that a person who had murdered someone with a Katana (Samurai Sword) knew I had swords and where they were kept.

To conclude I would rather still trust people and get caught than suspect everyone all the time.

Maybe I should adjust but not change.

My friend Albie says I should take the advice of a pipe smoker, look, think, have a puff of the pipe then make a decision.

I'm going to look on eBay for a pipe or six and that's alright as I have a book on how to stop smoking!

If I was psycho-analysed as to why I am the way I am, it may be possible that I felt inadequate as a child, just a thought, but maybe I am looking for an answer that is not there. Although most of what I had as a child was second hand, Colin (my brother) and I did not ever go without. It was the time, born in the baby boom, not too many years after the war – the Second World War not the first before anyone says anything regarding my age that I am touchy about!

Only recently did I discover that I am capable of more than I was told or thought I was. Looking back at School reports I was always criticised more than encouraged. I wrote my first book to try to encourage people with low self-esteem and called it *Ungifted*.

What I did not realise was that I had to work harder than most people.

Martial Arts, therapy (Shiatsu and Thai), all aspects I have reached a fair standard in, required me to read, study and train harder than my classmates to reach the same results.

I gave up learning French after studying for a couple of years – I could not pick it up, no wonder as I did not ever study in between lessons. The point is that I thought buying numerous books, CDs, DVDs were no good as I didn't listen to them!

I am at present trying to learn Japanese and play the guitar.

I was once told that if I ever got breathalysed, that the trick was to blow into the breathalyser like I was blowing into a flute. The idea was that not all of my breath would enter the monitor. Well if I was told this it must be true!!

One year, Kam, Kevin Brewerton and I took a group of students to train in Spain. We had a place in Torrevieja so it was easy to get another one for the students. In fact Alex Reid was part of Kevin's group who was later married to Katie Price (Jordan). I have a DVD of me sparring with him which I would love to share.

Each night we would go for a meal and end up in a bar near to where we were staying. As the bar was in the mountains, accessible by a windy road, drinking was not a problem; in fact the local Police would drop in and drink as well. This went on every night, but the problem was on the last night it occurred to me we would be driving back to Alicante airport in the early hours. I stopped drinking but was still over the limit by the time we had to leave. The car that we had hired had a registration plate that indicated they were hire cars, this coupled with the amount of equipment we had on the luggage rack made us a target to be stopped. Especially at four in the morning.

Yes we got pulled over the Spanish Police. In my opinion, the Spanish Police are more on the ball than ours (unfortunately). They checked my driving licence and details and asked me to blow into the breathalyser. Of course this did not bother me as I knew what to do! 'Again' the Police officer said as he was not satisfied so I repeated what I had done in the flute-like method. I had been told you could get away with the test if you blow into it like a flute. He got aggressive and pulled out a gun and demanded I do it properly. I did and somehow I passed, how I do not know, but I have never been over the limit since – well not too many times.

Fishing

Ever since I was a child, I have loved fishing. Again my equipment was basic and poor, like the old photo of the boy with a stick and hook. I have just managed to wean myself off spending more time and money in the tackle shops than fishing! I still come out of the shop with more than I needed but it is improving.

Fortunately I have never been a smoker or into drugs or I probably would have been an addict with an addictive personality. I like a beer but that is under control although I have been lucky as I have fallen asleep in ditches and been breathalysed in Spain when I was over the limit! so I count my blessings with that aspect of my life.

I have possibly one or two rods more than I need, but I think all fishermen do. I do however have slightly more pens, watches than I need but I do love writing books!

Fortunately I have never gambled only on the Grand National.

My Dad used to tell me stories of his straight laced Brother Sandy. He was the most charismatic man I had ever met and could charm the birds out of the trees. He had a mediocre job in an office and once went to the Dogs.

He became addicted to the point of borrowing petty cash from the office and on the audit day had to flush the receipts down the toilet. Later on in life he discovered the Jehovah witnesses and became obsessed with it much like me and with martial arts. I also love t shirts and got obsessed finding one.

I like buying one in every colour. This stopped when my tummy did not compliment them, possibly due to the three hernia operations I had or the occasional beer and Chinese!

Not unlike a dog who cannot resist stopping by a tree and going to the toilet. I cannot walk past a for sale sign whether it's a boat, car or dolls house.

It's no wonder I got obsessed with eBay, which was made for me.

Buying or bidding is so addictive, sensible people set a limit and stick to it but I then realise how much I want the item and cannot stop bidding!

I have bought some good and some bad and some that never turned up or looked nothing like their pictures, much like the dating sites!

The story that stands out for me is the Lego story. I asked my Daughter Lisa what I should buy for my Grandson George who had every toy available, she suggested a Lego set that was hard to get. I like a challenge and was so pleased when I found a new one on eBay and set about bidding. The bidding was going higher and higher but I could not give up and finally I won the item. I was pleased I phoned Lisa to tell her, who said she had tried to get one but the offers had got too high. Yes she was the other bidder! I will conclude this section as I am off to the post box to post a cheque too good to be true advert I have just read – how to stop being gullible send £100 to PO Box 6 Sunderland.

The Dating Game

When finishing with Clare, or should I say she finished with me, I jumped out of the frying pan into the fire.

Karen

Karen, a pretty blonde lady who I had known for several years and bumped into from time to time, was to become my comfort blanket.

She was attractive enough to want to be seen with, low maintenance, did not drink and had her own friends. This suited me down to the ground but it soon became apparent we did not have much in common and the conversations were shallow. We saw each other once to twice a week and this lasted about 18 months.

She was always well dressed and jolly but was convinced that I was still in love with Clare. This was true, but to say I would not go back with her was not wholly honest as I was missing her terribly but I did not miss the stress.

Shirly

Shirly, who I had met by chance in McDonalds one Sunday morning, had become a good friend and she would come round for a coffee and then a Chinese on a Friday night.

I actually like her and find her attractive with a good sense of humour. Unfortunately, she wants a platonic friendship which she made clear from the start.

Online

A couple of friends suggested that I join a dating site. I laughed initially as this was not for me.

I am now into my sixth week and it is emotionally draining. My ego and confidence rises and falls daily and mostly falls at the moment.

I had no idea how it worked or what to expect.

The first thing you do when you join is to put a profile and photos, and put what they think people want to read. I changed my photos like I would change the bait for fishing. Similar to fishing, you cast as many lines as possible.

Finding out the criteria is the first step when looking. Being shallow, the photo then the distance then finally interests and requirements.

Such things as not being bothered by looks is a lie, the first stumbling block was being under six foot. Everyone said good sense of humour but when I messaged a funny reply this did not stop me being deleted! Promising to answer all messages was another lie, a few replied to my first message then said I wasn't their type which does hurt as they were just being honest.

Becoming paranoid is a downside and a lack of patience and I suffer from both.

A watched kettle never boils and a watched phone does not ring! Or in this case does not make a noise that indicates you have a message or response. One of the hardest things to understand is when someone says they want to meet you then the messages suddenly dry up.

I can understand to a point that looking at a photo then deleting is natural but I deleted so many one night my finger hurt!

I also understand that when a couple meet and there is not any chemistry, when one does, and an excuse is made I find that hard to understand. I have a problem understanding when a phone call goes well and arrangements are made to meet then they cancel or don't get in touch. I accept this as one of life's mysteries.

I have been robbed three times by people I would have had to have known to make it possible and although I am not positive this drives me mad.

If I was cleverer, I would make a play or a film but for me this book may help someone else out – like an idiots guide to dating.

Meeting someone new didn't bother me as much as I thought, false opinion of myself, ego I do not know, but Teresea was a sought after person and Clare was attractive and 23 years younger, Karen was an ex-model. I went into the unknown confident – big mistake.

Sue from Hockley

My first reply was from a lady called Sue from Hockley. We spoke on the phone after a few messages, I prefer it that way. She was due to go to Australia for a few weeks so we arranged to meet for a coffee before she went to the Hawk in Battlesbridge. Feeling slightly apprehensive, we met inside. She looked like her photo and was pleasant to look at. We chatted and got on quite well. She owned a stable

and rode. The conversation flowed and although there was not great spark, I enjoyed her company. As she was to go away a few days later, I suggested that we meet the next day for a coffee, she declined as was busy but would email me about her trip on her return. She emailed but did not contact me on her return.

Ruth

Again as I followed up with a phone call to Ruth from Bishops Stortford, she seemed very pleasant. We arranged to meet on a Saturday for a drink near to where she lived. I was late as I had misjudged the distance. When I arrived I saw an attractive lady of 62. We got on well and stayed for a meal. When leaving she said she would not mind coming to my neck of the woods. Ruth came down on Monday and we got on well.

She invited me for dinner at her house the following Saturday and again we got on well.

We arranged to meet the following Saturday at a pub near to her house as my friend was playing in a band there. I suggested we could go for a Chinese after. All was set until Monday when she phoned and cancelled saying she was not ready for this.

You can check if someone is still active on the site which she was on. Ruth has been online since.

Confused.com

I was contacted again, this time by a lady from Brentwood. We spent some time speaking on the phone. She was funny and jolly so we arranged to meet for a coffee and had a fun hour. I was not sure of my attraction to her but was sure she was attracted to me. We met again on Sunday and she had lunch with me and my grandson George. She was a nice person and I wish I was attracted to her but unfortunately I wasn't and I think she knew this. We said goodbye and no further arrangements were made.

Sue from Colchester

Profile said mad, quirky – when we spoke I asked if I had the wrong number. Luckily she was ok with my sarcasm. We met up, she was quite attractive and had a nice personality. We had a coffee and she came back to mine for another coffee. She cancelled the next date then re-arranged. We met for lunch and she came back for another coffee. Not sure if she was moody, unwell or had a dry sense of humour. She cancelled our next date and said she would ring – still waiting, confused.com again

Sue from Colchester with horses

Spoke, she sounded educated, was an editor and had horses and dogs. We met for dinner. She was not at all like the photo. She was a nice person and asked many questions but the shallow side of me did not find her attractive. We said goodbye and she offered to edit my book for me.

Sandie from Southend

Again another horse person, she writes for a living. We met at Battlesbridge, she looked better than her photo and was chatty – I thought we got on well, we arranged another date that she cancelled, she said she would call to re-arrange. Still waiting.

Jan
The confusing part again, long nice message from Jan from Southend, had a date booked for next Wednesday but she has cancelled as had another date before and said this had gone well.

Sue from Hockley
Is back from Australia and wants to meet again

Laurel Chelmsford Teacher
Exchanged several texts but does not get my sense of humour, possibly meeting for a coffee.

Several messages from women wanting to meet but being shallow and seeing their photos I deleted them.

Sue from Hockley
Phoned and we met at the Hawk. Got on much better this time and she came back to mine for coffee. I have been seeing her for five months and thought it was going well until I came out of hospital after a Hernia operation. She picked me up from the hospital but hasn't been there for me as much as I would have hoped. Probably too much time on my own to think but felt she could have been there more so I am pulling back and acting indifferent.

August 15th 2015

As I am writing several years later I cannot remember names but I'll do my best.

Lady from Islington, foolishly drove, took hours to get there and it was difficult to park, meeting an average plump lady in a pub where neither of us seemed very keen, not a bad thing if I wouldn't want to drive back there again.

If she had seemed keener I may have wanted to meet again.

Wondering what to wear is another question before these dates, not wanting to wear a suit but not being scruffy and not smart enough.

I went by train to meet a lady from Finchley who to my surprise was petite and attractive – she was the Mum of one of the Spice Girls, Emma Bunton (Pauline) and looked like she could have been in the group.

We met up again and she asked to read a draft copy of my book. Before our third date she called to say I was not for her but would return my book. This time I made less effort and wore jeans. We had coffee. She said she was used to dating men with better dress sense and wearing suits, but said I looked better this time.

Thinking this is not for me and making less effort seems to be more attractive.

I was contacted by a few women and met for a coffee, one offered to re-write my profile for me as said I should be more honest with what I wanted and she was right.

Another asked if she could come to see my mobile home as she said was thinking of getting one but made it clear there would be no hanky panky. As I had just come off of hospital that was the last thing on my mind but clearly not on hers. I had to decline the offer as I had stitches in.

The problem with this blind dating is guilt. When meeting someone naturally that is outside of internet dating sites, if the chemistry is there whether physical or personality, one goes forward for what could be a permanent relationship or until the sparkle vanishes. But when meeting someone on a dating site with an arranged date it is difficult to go to the next level. Polite people don't show disappointment and thick skinned people don't pick up on when it's not right. I have experienced both and I have been disappointed they haven't liked me.

Fake or dated photos

I arranged to meet a lady from Colchester in an Asda cafe one Sunday afternoon – I know how to treat a lady. After the drive I saw an elderly lady, pleasant enough but it was like sitting with my elderly Aunt. Thankfully they were closing – say no more.

I arranged to meet an Indian lady at the festival leisure park in Basildon, whilst waiting I started to get a bit panicky. Eventually she arrived, not unattractive but with no fireworks. As we spoke she did seem to become more attractive. We had a mutual friend – Brinsley, her son had worked as a lighting engineer for.She owned a Beauty parlour in Leigh. I asked her if she fancied another date but she politely declined my offer.

That would have been bad enough but when I mentioned to Brinsley he nearly choked on his coffee saying she owned a massage parlour and was as we say a professional lady!

So I had been turned down by a professional lady – things could only get better.

I thought I had come off the site, but my profile must have still been active as Jacqui contacted me. She knew who I was but I didn't remember her. Apparently she and her Brother Brian had trained under me in Karate years ago. We met at the Harvester for a meal and got on very well. We started to see each other on a regular basis and became a couple – this lasted for four years.

Jacqui was extremely supportive of my ventures and stood by me with all my ventures and misadventures. She was a very kind person who looked after me when I had a hip operation. One of our ventures was to buy a caravan in Weeley Bridge park. She looked after the bookings and we had a lot of regular weekend breaks there. One of my good friends Richard rented it off me and decided to buy one of his own, sharing many a weekend with us. Unfortunately, I did not seem to give Jacqui what she needed and she accused me of seeing Clare what was untrue.

Whether this was the real reason she decided to end our relationship remains a mystery. I say mystery but as Jacqui and Richard are now a fully fledged couple I guess there is no mystery!

I am not going back to internet dating, I will let fate take it hand. I do feel a bit sad as we had some good times, but the guilt I initially felt has now gone as they seem happy and in love. Jacqui was also a very possessive person who seemed to fall out with a lot of people – especially anyone who gave me any attention including my family which did make things awkward and looking back I do feel a lot freer, I am not someone who likes to be controlled and it later came to light that she had been reading my phone and blocking many of my contacts – I feel better for now being single but watch this space!

Guitar

Richard, my ex-friend and Jacqui, my ex-girlfriend and I, decided to do a boot sale in Wheeley where my caravan is. The boot sale in Wheeley was a lot smaller than the local ones I was used to. As I said earlier, the dynamics between Richard and Jacqui worked well – too well it would seem! Richard is a multi-talented person who can play the Guitar to a very high standard.

Richard and I were walking around leaving Jacqui to mind the stall, her words to me were "Don't come back with any junk! I spotted a nice looking guitar on a stall, the owner must have been tipped off I was coming as he said you look like a rock star. You should have this guitar...I think he had almost finished his sentence before I bought it. Richard said it was OK and he would teach me to play saying it would be a piece of cake – maybe he meant rock cake! He was generous to fault, fitting new strings – this continued after Jacqui and I split up. The confusing part was that he would continuously tell me that she was too controlling and demanding and he said, rolling his eyes, that she would phone him, slagging me off and meeting him for coffee. She did leave me a letter saying she would give me another chance if I agreed to her terms and conditions including seeing a therapist for my large ego!

I got a phone call from Richard sounding distressed, which bothered me as he had recently suffered a heart attack. But the reason for the call and the nervous sound in his voice, was to tell me that he and Jacqui were as he put 'An item'.

Although I had never met up with any of my ex-partners when I was with Jacqui, I have since met with Clare for a coffee and Shirly. I actually think Jacqui and Richard make a good couple – not sour grapes, just being honest.

Words

Over the years I have discovered, eventually, that words do not always mean what they say

Definitely – *probably especially with enquiries*

One Careful owner – *Poßibly many but one was careful*

You're the first – *tonight!*

Money back – *no chance*

The last one – *on the counter*

Simple Guide – *if your a genius*

I will call you tonight – *If I feel like it!*

Lifetime guarantee – *Depends on how long you live*

One coat of paint – *If you put it on with a trowel*

It won't hurt – *Not for the person inflicting the pain*

Teeth whitening toothpaste – *After how long?*

It hurts me more than it hurts you – *Well don't do it then!*

It is for your own good – *and theirs!*

Not being personal but – *no your being nosey and blunt*

I'm broke – *In your pocket not your bank*

Just a thought – *If poison goes out of its sell by date is it still poisonous?!*

I am now having Guitar lessons once a week and taking advice from friends who play the Guitar. I have updated my Guitar to a suitable one or should I say four! Plus a superb electric one that Stephe and Glenn bought me for my Birthday.

More easy to play DVDs and books – easy perhaps for Eric Clapton, but I enjoy the challenge and losing myself for an hour a day not thinking of Martial arts or other aspects of my life. At the moment the only person who recognises my songs is my Daughter Lisa – but I think she notices the song sheets!

As I have said many times, there is no order to this book as I write things as they happen or come into my head.

Recently, I went into hospital for a small operation for Bursitis – having false hips the simple injection has to be done under Anaesthetic. As I lay in the theatre my name was called and to my surprise the man on the bed next to me said is that Karate Jim? We could not see each other as we were both lying down, but started a conversation. His name was Dave Griggs so there is another story. Before moving to Orsett, which was our last family home, we lived in Malvern Road in Grays. It was a large double fronted house with two sellers – see my autobiography for other stories. We wanted a porch fitted and for once I contacted several builders for estimates. I even got the price down, which shocked Teresea. Dave Griggs got the job – a nice man who eventually made a decent job of the porch. Teresea had to scrape all of the varnish off the bullseye windows, but not bad.

As he was fair and a nice person, we decided to have a small conservatory built on the back and used Dave again. This time it was a different kettle of fish. He came in the morning and either started part of the job or made a token visit saying he was going to get materials for the jobs. He sometimes came back the same day but mostly would go missing for up to a week, Teresea was getting annoyed and blamed me. Meanwhile my Brother Colin had returned home from one of his ventures, mainly in America. He was like the Prodigal Son for the first week but this would then wear off and he would borrow my Dad's car and return it with no petrol. My dad would have to go straight to the petrol station or would run out of fuel. Colin would eat my parents out of the house and home. Colin was getting bored and still felt suffocated by my Mum and Dad. I must admit they were over protective and although Colin had lived rough and travelled to un-usual places, they still gave him restrictions.

I had a brain wave – I could get Colin to work for Dave. Colin is very handy and hard working. Everyone was happy – for a short time.

I was sitting in my living room feeling pleased with myself, gloating, until what can only be described as mayhem: Colin and the builder were fighting in the garden! I flipped, ran out – they both ran off leaving all the tools – so my good idea turned out to be a bad one! The job did eventually get finished and I never saw Dave again until the Hospital.

Another time that getting friends to do jobs went wrong, was when we moved to Long Lane. Long Lane was a lovely, Tudor type chalet Bungalow. After a long persistent journey we eventually moved in.

It was owned by an old man – Mr Deadman It was a 1925 property that needed lots of work to update it. Looking back it would have been better to have left a lot of the original features such as the fireplace and the bathroom because they then became retro and fashionable years later.

The first thing Teresea wanted, was to get the central heating installed. Teresea's Uncle Bill who worked at Proctor and Gamble said Danny the maintenance fitter was very good at installing central heating.

Danny, well to say Danny was slow was an understatement! He would come straight from work, get his tools out then have his sandwiches and a cup of tea and sometimes did something but would normally spend the first hour talking. It was not uncommon for him to eat his sandwiches, drink his tea then say it was not worth starting and leave. I also think he had a fascination for Teresea not helped by her sitting there speaking to him. It took months to almost finish, I say almost as I got the hump in the end and gave him his marching orders. I had to finish the job myself and anyone who knows about my

DIY skills will disbelieve this bit but somehow I did finish it.

We had a few other disasters when we lived in Long lane, but the one that comes to mind is when we decided to have a patio and ornamental wall put up in the garden.

Again, I was recommended to use Colin – a man who used to work with my Dad. My dad had seen Colin's work in his own house. I actually went to see his work before asking him to undertake my project. It was just as my Dad described, the problem was that Colin did not know what to charge. We agreed on a daily rate, which was reasonable. But Colin was a perfectionist. He was also very slow hence the cost was a lot more by the time it was finished. He did a superb job but by the time it was finished we had decided to sell the house due to it being a two bedroom property and our request for an extension had been turned down. I would say the lovely garden with the ornamental wall helped to sell the house, but when the buyers came to move in they had not realised there was a patio and decorative wall. Going back to my extension story I don't think I would have believed some of my stories if I was told them by someone else.

The chalet bungalow was a Tudor type with the bedrooms in the roof. As we were planning on having a second child, we needed another bedroom. The only way we could have an extension was to have a room built on stilts over the drive. I had seen something like this when going to my Karate class – the house was on the old A13 next to the Linford turn off. So one day after my class I went and knocked on the house and a lady with only a towel wrapped around her opened the door. I quickly explained my reason for the visit – she was very friendly and offered to show me around. Feeling a little uncomfortable she showed me the bedroom when I heard someone call out, Are you up there? Whose car is that?

The bedroom door opened and the lady's husband walked in – he looked at me, not sure what to think. To my amazement he believed my quick explanation and gave me details of the Architect who had designed his and even offered me a cup of tea which I declined and thanked my lucky stars.

Van

Some years ago I thought about getting a van and having it written both to carry my equipment and for advertising. For some time Clare used it which was OK as it was advertising my schools.

My Son Ian called one day and said he was looking out of his office window and saw a vintage Bakers van painted in my colours, black and red. He sent me a photo and it looked interesting. Something out of Foyles' War or older. It was in fact a converted London Taxi. I phoned the person selling it and made an offer which he accepted. The only problem was that Ian lived close to the Scottish border, North of Newcastle.

But this was not a problem, it was an adventure. I caught the train to Ian's and stayed the night. I took Ian's twins out, had some photos taken with them and prepared for the journey home. The van was surprisingly comfortable. My first problem was I took the wrong turn and ended up heading for Scotland. I travelled for ten miles then realised I had gone the wrong way and headed back in the right direction.

The journey took me ten hours and I eventually got home with very dim headlights. The van does not get used much as I have a small collection of cars and it stands outside my DOJO most of the time. But it has been useful when buying bits to renovate my disastrous properties. The strange thing is as it is so old it does not need an MOT.

My good friend and long suffering patient Brian Spurrin, affectionately known as Brian the Carpet man, is one of the nicest men I have ever known.

He has a bed and carpet shop in Grays that he has owned for over fifty years. Everyone knows Brian and he knows everyone. Unfortunately Grays has declined in many ways, coupled with the necessity to have shutters fitted and the famous fish and chip shop next door Mumfords closing, Brian decided not to renew his lease. Brian very kindly offered me and my family some of his stock including beds and mattresses. As mentioned earlier, I bought a caravan in Wheeley and due to unforeseen circumstances I no longer use it and rent it out. Lisa markets it and she suggested I get a new bed as the current one was very uncomfortable. So the opportunity to have a new bed was perfect timing. My plan was to collect

the bed from Brian one Saturday. I made sure the battery was charged. Meanwhile one of my black belts suffers from depression and asked if we could meet up and have a chat. As chief instructor and Therapist this is not unusual but sometimes can be a bit draining if I see three or four negative people in a row.

I suggested, as time is a commodity, we meet at the end of the lesson and he came with me to collect the bed and we could then talk. Whilst there, another student arrived and said he would also come with us and help load the mattress. Derek also suffers with depression and low self-esteem.

All was going well, we loaded the mattress onto the van and Derek was also given a mattress – Brian suggested we

put his mattress on top of mine on the van. Everyone was happy, when BANG! The suspension collapsed in the middle of the road outside a bus stop. So I stopped the traffic and had two less than positive people with me – Derek and Mark had now become friends, which was just as well as they had to carry Derek's mattress to his house a mile or so away. I called the AA and explained a low loader would be needed to recover my van. An hour passed when a small AA van turned up, the driver started to have a go at me then realised the situation. I eventually got a low loader to take my van back to my DOJO. Ian has shown interest in the van and would like to change it into a camper van so he is planning to come down to Essex and drive it back to Newcastle – in reverse of when I collected it.

Fishing Magazines

Brilliant is the only way to describe the way they combine articles with marketing. Top anglers really know their onions. They are top because they are good at catching fish. Firstly they know where to fish and what equipment and bait to use. However they do advocate that the manufacturer of the products who is paying them are the best. This could be true or a twin edged sword. The magazines are filled with wonder bait. I know I am an Angler and believe things, knowing what works in different circumstances is the art.

Buying magazines and equipment is one of my hobbies, I even have ten rods in my shed!

Martial Arts

Martial Arts, a subject I do know something about. Having studied for over fifty years and being lucky enough to have travelled around the world training with the best instructors, gives me the right to give my opinions. But I must add that opinions are just that. How each person sees something. I am an acquired taste as is my Martial Arts. I suggest anyone thinking of taking up martial Arts looks at a few classes. Find the cost and check out the instructors credentials such as how long they have been training. All martial arts can be very different in style but all have their own benefits. It is what the individual is looking for. When first starting Karate, I had only seen it in a James Bond film, the style I trained in was not competition based but I did enter a competition after a year. I was misinformed and believed my basic training would come naturally in the competition. Rubbish! The opponents were conditioned experienced competitors. I lost all but one of the fights sustaining a fat lip that resembled the African tribe that put saucers in their lips. I did not realise how fat it was until I went to work thinking no one would notice – big mistake. All of my work colleagues put tissue paper in their mouths and asked me how I got on.

Albie was not only my first black belt but a very close friend too. Albie and I have one other thing in common – being obsessive and buying. We both came up with a scheme as we both bought training books, aids and equipment, we assumed others would do the same. So we purchased track suits, books and various training items to sell. We stored them in my cellar but we did not think of the damp. Nevertheless we got rid of most of the goods with no profit but got us interested in other aspects of selling.

Toys were one of the ventures, but this failed as the toys got either broken or ruined at the Toy parties we ran which meant no profit.

Seriously Wrong

One time that I seriously misjudged a student, was a few years ago.

I wrote this story in my book *The Journey*. In the book I changed the person's name but it was a guy called Dave.

I liked Dave, he was a bodybuilder and very talented in Kick-boxing.He would show off a bit as he had very flamboyant kicks.

The week before the incident I am going to write about, Dave and I had a beer together after my Karate class. He opened up to me as it was just him and I. Dave also spoke of his love of music, especially the Piano. He came across as a nice family man who loved both his wife and daughter. I must admit, some of my instructors saw something that I didn't, what transpired showed they were right.

On the Tuesday which followed my drink with Dave, I ran a kick-boxing class in the Eversley Centre in Pitsea and at the end he approached me as he wanted to ask me a question. The question was would I teach Dave's daughter martial Arts when she was older. He said that he liked my etiquette. I agreed but as she was very young I said we could talk about it again at a later date.

Dave left the centre and I had a coffee before going on to my next class which was in Horndon. As I was about to leave, I heard some commotion in the car park.The doors were locked preventing me from leaving. The Police had arrived, a police helicopter and several armed Police officers.

One of the Police officers came in and recognised me and asked if I taught Dave. To say I was shocked with what he said next would be an understatement.

What he told me was unofficial, but as he knew me gave me some information as to what was going on. He firstly asked me if I taught anyone to use weapons. The Police officer then told me that Dave had been arrested.

As Dave had Nunchaku on him, I was asked if I taught him how to use them. Of course I did, but at the time I did not see the significance.

Dave not only trained with the Nunchakus but also with the Katana (Japanese Samurai sword). In fact he had been lent a Katana by Stephe Jones, one of my instructors.

What actually happened was one of the most horrific things I have ever heard. Although I didn't know the details that night, I was to then read about it in the newspapers. Dave had locked up his wife and his child in his loft for three weeks. Not only locked up but beaten his wife with some weapons, possibly the Nunchaku I had taught him to use.

The Police said that the injuries inflicted on his wife,

were the worst that they had ever seen. The photos in the newspapers showed them.

He was convicted and put away for nine years – possibly more as the court broke down the charges so they could be run consecutively to each other. The only way that Dave's wife had escaped, was that she had managed to smuggle in her phone in her baby's bag.

Stansted

When I had my cottage in Brittany, Clare and I would take regular breaks there. I thought it would be a nice gesture to invite her mum and dad one time and this would give me the opportunity to impress them.

At the time President Bush was coming over and extra security was at Stansted Airport.

As my suitcase was going through the hand luggage scanner, there was a look of concern on the lady operating the x-ray machine. She stopped the conveyor and picked up the phone. I stood there, anxious but waited patiently.

The next thing I know, two armed Police Officers came and arrested me and took me away. The x-ray machine had shown a knife in my case, not just any knife, but a flick knife. On a previous trip, I had bought two flick knives, one for me and one as a present for my karate instructor Bob Lawrence. He had suffered a stroke and could only use one hand. Foolishly I left my one in the case.

I was taken to a room and questioned by the Police Officers. They called their superior officers to come in.

A female police officer came in, wearing armour and carrying a machine gun, fully prepared to deal with a 'terrorist'.

I was getting anxious with the situation and knowing Clare and her parents were waiting in the secured part of the airport didn't help me either.

The female officer looked at me intensely, then said 'Oh my god, it's Jim McAllister!' She not only knew me, she was also one of my instructors students, Dawn.

She assured her colleagues that I said who I said I was and allowed me to continue my trip on the proviso I checked in on my return, minus the knife. Thanks Dawn.

Close shave

One venture was when I nearly bought a fitness studio in Southend-on-Sea. Gary Hogben, one of my instructors and long term friend, was having a sun-bed in a fitness studio which was spread over three floors and overheard the owner saying he intended to sell it. As soon as Gary finished his sun-bed he phoned me – he was the one who suggested I call my schools the Jim McAllister School of Martial Arts and later Academy.

I initially contacted the owner – John Arthur – to see if this was the case, which he confirmed and we arranged to meet up. Surprisingly, Teresea was also on board with the idea and came with me.

He was a nice enough man who told us what we wanted to hear. My idea was to get a loan from the bank and convert part of the premises into a dojo, rent it to other people for Martial Arts classes to pay for the loan and also make a good profit. I even planned to take my Mum and Dad on board to run the daytime part. I was still working for Murco. Everything seemed to be coming together and I was in the proceeds of securing the loan. We were due to go to Torrevieja in our place in

Spain for a couple of weeks. The irony was that John's parents lived in Spain close to where our house was. We arranged to meet them and they were a very nice couple but when we told them our intentions they showed slight concern. It was not what they said, but what they did not that concerned us.

When we returned to England, I could not wait to start preparing for the new venture. One of my friends knew someone who owned a paper shop a few doors away who told him a Karate man from Grays was buying the Gym. I started to buy things for the gym. My Mum and Dad were getting excited, but for some reason things did not seem like they did at the beginning. Fortunately, before money was exchanged, a few things came to light. Years before I had gone to train in Malaysia on the recommendation of a local dentist – the connection was that his Brother had trained with the local champion Johnny Lowe and when I was there I met one of his students – Nathan. Recently I had met up with him who had come to live in the UK and became Friends with a good friend of mine – Tony Childs. The ironic thing was that Nathan was a dark black man who sold sunbeds! On meeting him I told him of my venture, then he told me that the gym was not John Arthur's to sell. Strangely enough John then seemed to vanish. What was also strange was that Master Loke – a well known Tang-Su-Do Teacher (Korean style) from Grays, was also buying it from John Arthur – hence the Karate man from Grays was both of us! Years later I also found out from my friend Brinsley whose Dad owned TOTS nightclub, that he was a known con-man who used to frequent the nightclub and this was also confirmed by Neil Cooper, a friend of mine.

Dad's Car

I have explained some bits about my parents but a quick synopsis of my Dad would be that he was a thoughtful, kind and generous man with a nasty temper and I miss him terribly.

When I passed my driving test Dad would let me borrow his car. The first accident I had in his Morris Minor, I got away with, as he did not notice the damage, but the second one was slightly different. Dad had bought a Zephyr, it was a flashy young man's car – according to my Mum! One night when I was working in Chadwell garage – yes me working in a garage! I had completed my short course on motor mechanics at Letchworth Government Training Centre. Johnny Deuce, the foreman invited a few of us to go out to a pub. John knew a lot of people and places. One of the fitters, Derek was invited too and had had recently bought a sunbeam rapier in pristine condition. Derek was not the most charismatic man but was a good mechanic who loved his car. In fact he spent most of his time polishing and cleaning it when he was not working.

John was in the firm's van leading the group. Derek

was with his fat friend Billy (I used to tell people his surname was Hunter – similar to Bunter out of the comics) – I followed on with my arm around a girl, showing off, as the car had a bench seat. We raced round the lanes trying to keep up with the car in front. This was until the road works and traffic lights, John stopped, Derek stopped and I stopped – after driving into Derek's pride and joy. Dad's car now had a slight alteration to the front wing. When I got home, I woke Dad to tell him what had happened. Knowing I was not hurt, he went back to sleep. I went back out as Betty, the pump lady at the garage, was having a party at the caravan she lived in. When I came home the following morning, Mum told me that Dad was less than pleased with me. Dad had looked at the car and when noticing the little damage had said a few choice words (Dad although an ex-marine and worked in the docks)never said anything stronger than Bloody at home, he also threw the keys up the garden. By the time I got home he had calmed down and I assured him I would get it repaired – yes I was recommended to someone who would do it cheap! Yes he did replace the wing but the colour he sprayed it with did not quite match the rest of the car – the car was an off white , the wing was bright white but it was OK as the repair man assured me it would fade. The only thing that faded eventually was Dad's disappointment and he did continue to let me borrow his car. I eventually bought my own car, a sit up and Beg Ford.

I recently saw a photo of Angela, a previous girlfriend, sitting in a mobility scooter and contacted her to say it would be safer than when she fell out of my sit up and begcar when going around a corner and the door opened. I'm not sure if the lucky escape was not getting injured or her not being with me! She said not completely, re-minding me when I accidentally knocked her out cold whilst doing the conga at a friends party.

Flashy cars

Ok I have an ego, in fact Jacqui said if I wanted her back I needed to get therapy to get rid of my inflated ego. When I told my Son this he said there is not a therapist qualified enough to do this.

What does someone with an inflated ego drive ?

I have champagne taste and beer money as my dear old friend Johnny Wiggins used to say.

This is what dodgy car repairs do to make money, (Johnny Wiggins) they buy, write off cars, repair and sell them. My problem solved – a Porsche, get some registration plates and away I go. LJI 603 from Ireland – Lisa Jim and Ian of course. It did get attention and comments from the people I worked with. All was fine and it gave me street cred when I was organising the Kick boxing shows. Well until one show I put on at the civic hall in Grays with lots of razzmatazz.

One aspect was the ring girls. On this occasion I went over the top as I knew someone who was the agent for the models from the Sunday sport newspaper who were glamorous, scantily dressed and entertaining. I paid their fees at the end of the night but unfortunately their lift

did not turn up to take them home. The girls lived in London and this was the days before mobile phones, so I had the responsibility of getting the girls home. I explained this to my wife Teresea who strangely accepted it – I had to somehow squeeze three nearly naked women into my Porsche! I also had to put my case full of the money in the back. It was one in the morning when I got stopped by the Police. Unbeknown to me the boot had come undone, probably due to the amount of people in the car, and being a cut and shut Johny Wiggins special, the case had come undone and money was blowing out of the car. It looked like they were ladies of the night with me as their pimp in my dodgy suit. Luckily I had not been drinking. The police let us go but the girls could not remember their address. I eventually got home at four in the morning to a less than happy wife. I am not sure I would have believed the story.

Books

I personally never thought that I would write a book not being particularly academic and a bit dyslexic as a child. However, I have now written eight books.

It all started when my friend Geoff Langham after hearing my stories said – you should write a book. I did just that, my autobiography called *Ungifted*.

Since then I have written a story part fiction called *The Journey*. I have also written a few books on Martial Arts including the *Jim McAllister Encyclopaedia on Martial Arts*.

Unfortunately I never completed my friend Billy Blundell's autobiography as he sadly died before I could finish it. Eddy, Bill's brother also a friend of mine, did however manage to write his book which sold many copies.

At the moment I am reading Colin Picketts' life story which makes mine look like an Enid Blyton book!

Even if publishing it is not the goal, the satisfaction is cathartic and worth the time, I promise.

It is nice to leave a legacy for our families and in my case also for my students. It is amazing what one can

achieve when we put our minds to it but remember work comes before success only in the dictionary.

Thank you to my Daughter Lisa for patiently deciphering my writing and spell checking and for typing without prejudice or judging me, sorry Lis you are a chip of the old block!

Humour

Humour in a relationship can be a tricky thing.

Most of my male friends share a similar sense of humour, obviously we have our preferred comedians especially as I am older than most of them. I don't find new ones that over swear that are funny, but on the same yardstick I do find Billy Connolly and Jim Davidson funny. Ok I am a bit of a hypocrite as I mentioned earlier!

Women and humour, well that's another subject. I have not met too many women that make me laugh. In fact I can probably name them.

Teresea shared the same humour as me initially, but became a bit more serious as the years went on. This may have been from living with me or her role as a Counsellor may have had something to do with it. We now see each other at Christmas and the Grandchildren's birthdays and I see her interact with them, as she used to with me.

Clare was and still is a very funny lady, who not only got me but gave me a good run for my money.

Karen sometimes missed the point – enough said!

Lisa has the same sense of humour as me and a bit more. She has the ability to say funny things without realising it.

Shirly can be extremely funny.

Connie was naturally funny.

Lisa's friend Vikki also makes me laugh.

I recently got a call from an old friend I had not seen for years – Maxine.

Maxine laughs a lot and has a terrific sense of humour and like Lisa has the ability to tell a good story.

We met for a coffee and had a much needed laugh. What with my year and her loss of Paul, her husband, who sadly died two years ago of cancer.

The common denominator with most of my friends male and female, is the ability to laugh at themselves.

In my opinion, women's sense of humour is to detect when the laugh is genuine or flirty. I also find it hard to understand when a comedian comes on stage and says a few F words and the audience busts up.

I know Tommy Cooper could just come on stage and without saying anything the audience would be in stitches, but he was an exception and a genius.

So to summarise, humour is important in a woman to me, but no matter how funny Hatty Jacques is, I would pick Barbara Windsor to be with!

Likewise, if Brad Pitt and Ken Dood were in a bar having a beer and a lady came in who would she pick? Brad not known for his humour would likely win and hopefully Ken Dodd would find it funny!

Trust

Powerful subject I know and I am not going to stand on the moral ground.

I have done things wrong and paid the price. My infidelity lost and hurt Teresea terribly and destroyed my relationship with my children for some time, as well as losing the house I worked so hard for.

I will always have a sense of guilt. The reason I write this is to endorse that I have been accused of cheating in the past which was not true. So what I am writing may seem hypocritical but maybe it is Karma, as what goes around comes around.

I have been robbed twice by people I must have known and have been hurt by finding out people have gone through my phone. My friend Billy Blundell said he avoided prison for many things he did but got sent down for things he did not – so perhaps I should stop whinging.

2022 – What a Year

It started with my break up with Jacqui. As mentioned before in this book. Then shortly after I got the news that my good friend Dave Phillips suddenly died. Dave and I shared the same love of Martial Arts but had different views of the Art. We often had heated discussions but in the end we agreed to differ. I was both shocked and saddened to hear the news.

Craig, his son, asked if I wanted to read the Eulogy. This was difficult, not because of the public speaking as I have done lots of that in my life – not bad for a person who as a

boy suffered with a bad stutter and low self-esteem. The reason it was difficult was that Dave's parents were in the front row facing me and obviously in a bad way. To add insult to injury, also facing me were Shirly and Jacqui.

Shirly and Jacqui had never met up until that point but both knew Dave through me and shared a common dislike for each other.

Shortly after losing Dave, I got the sad news that my Aunty Rhoda had sadly passed in her sleep. Although sad as with all bereavements, it was in fact kind as she had sadly declined in both mental and physical health. Nevertheless I had lost my Aunty. I used to visit her in a care home firstly in Sandy then in Luton and would take my other Aunty – Connie with me.

Both Rhoda (my Dad's sister) and Connie (my mum's sister) knew each other well as both were evacuated to Biggleswade during the war.

The only difficult part was the funeral, as my cousin Jean was going to be there.I don't not like many people but I do have a dislike for Jean. (Ok I am not keen on Rylan!)] I felt wronged as she would criticise me for not hoovering Rhoda's apartment in the care home and all the things I did not do on my visits. Not once did she ever give me any praise – not that I wanted praise but I certainly did not want criticism! The journey took two hours each way and petrol and when Rhoda was able I would take her shopping and for lunch, what with a new tyre this added up.

I was, apart from Derek, the one who visited on a regular basis and the only problem this gave me was the criticism and hypocrisy which I hate with a passion. I managed to distant myself at the wake to avoid any falseness or hypocrisy.

Connie was not only my Aunt but also my godmother. She was a smart lady with a great sense of humour. Lisa saw her as Aunty as opposed to her Great Aunt. Connie was ninety but looked much younger and was switched on. Visiting Rhoda with her over the last ten years bought us much closer.

I would torment and play tricks on her which she enjoyed.

When Connie was taken into hospital, I visited her and noticed a considerable change in her appearance. This may have been because she didn't have makeup on and her hair wasn't done or maybe she was just ready to leave.

Connie, although she had a son who did everything for her, was lonely and didn't want to go back to her immaculate mobile home as she was getting depressed, so when I got the news I was very upset but in a funny way was pleased she had passed away rather than live a lonely life.

Vic was my cousin but so much more. It would not be possible to describe Vic without writing a book on him. Handsome, charismatic, funny would all be words I would use to give a brief summary. Vic was older than me and my hero. He had a leather import business and a wonderful family who he doted on. He lived in a large detached house in Kent.

Vic was my squash partner, drinking partner and confident. I got a phone call from Matt – Vic's son and my 'second son'. He said Jim I have some tragic news, Dad's just died.

Words cannot describe my shock – I am still in shock.

I could go on and on about Vic but I put Vic's history to show how much this coupled with the other events added to my disastrous year.

Martial Arts is not a sport but a way of life, so it is natural that Teachers, training partners and students become an extended family.

I understand when students leave – either they no longer want to train or take another path. However, I always get saddened. By the same yardstick, I am honoured and privileged to have students that either still train with me or keep in touch after many years – almost fifty in some cases.

Tony Childs was one such student. Tony trained with me for many years, was one of my first black belts and part of my dream team. Tony wanted to study one of the old styles of Karate and for some years went in this direction. He became head of his association and was one of England's top instructors. Tony and I had also shared many adventures outside of Karate.

Tony always kept in touch and a couple of years ago he started training with me again which I was happy about.

Tony, alongside Phil Hibert, who again resumed training with me, would come round my house on a Tuesday and train in various aspects of Martial Arts. Shaun, one of Tony's friends and students, would also join us.

Pat Drake, a top jiu-jitsu martial Artist, joined our small group teaching us once a month.

Phil is an identical twin to Kevin, who had been diagnosed with prostate cancer. As Phil shared the same DNA, was advised to go and have a check up. Although he had no symptoms, was also found to have the same prostate cancer as Kevin. After both Phil and Kevin had successfully recovered from their operations, Phil returned to training on a Tuesday. He suggested to Tony that he went for a check up.

Tony was diagnosed with the same prostate disease as Phil and Kevin, Tony was immediately admitted to hospital for the same operation,

A couple of days later, Tony phoned me from his hospital bed saying he would be out shortly and I was welcome to visit him – in other words, would I visit him. I decided to give him a surprise visit that day but on my way, one of his close friends, Robbie Curtis phoned me to say he had been taken into intensive care and was not allowed visitors. My next call was to say that he had suffered a heart attack on his way to the bathroom and died. Like with Vic, I am still in shock. Tony was a person with strong opinions, liked a beer, generous to a fault with a dry sense of humour.

Tuesdays would never be quite the same again without my friend and student.

Although I had a lovely stress free Christmas with my family, I was glad to see the end of 2022.

Pal, an Indian Sikh, also a chemist and scientist, had a few years ago invited Shirly and I for dinner. A very interesting and knowledgeable man who I had met at Steve Knight's birthday.Wrongly I never returned the favour of keeping in touch, maybe due to my changing circumstances.

Just before Christmas, I received an invitation for myself , Kam , Rose and Shirly to go for dinner. Neither Shirly or Rose wanted to go so just Kam and I took up the invitation. Without going into boring detail, my phone was not getting messages and I got to Pal's house first. The only reason I am giving this backdrop is because this next part changed part of my life. Pal took the opportunity of me being there first to show me around his large and interesting house. Whilst he was showing me his son's bedroom with a four poster bed and lots of hand made wooden furniture , I spotted a book.

Pal's phone rang and I had a crafty look at the book.

'You can have it '

He said when he came back, I had been gingerly looking at the book and had not noticed he had finished his call.

Anyone who has read the book or seen the film Hurricane will be able to relate to the phrase, you do not find books, books finds you. Well this was certainly the case. The book was called *Make It Happen*.

It is a sort of self help book not dissimilar to what I have read before, but the difference was it was written for me. Well not literally but in my words and humour.

The author explained the formula to manifest things and was not frightened to disclose her own experiences , both good and bad. She suggested that the reader who wants change in their life, needs to do something about it, Firstly writing a list of what they actually want. After finishing the book I decided to do just that.

So what do I want? Not a lot-sounds like Paul Daniels!

well not actually true, but not the same as what I would have written in my earlier life.

I have a good family and a large circle of friends. I like where I live – Ok I don't own my place like most people of my age but I am not like most people of my age!

I do sail close to the wind with money but always manage to find a breeze. I have more cars, fishing rods and clothes that I need. I can afford to go on holiday and to socialise.

So what do I want or need? As long as my properties that I sort of own, gives me enough income and with my pension to pay my rent, I'm happy. Massage and teaching Martial Arts, tops up the rest and somehow I manage to afford to run my cars and a social life, how I don't know – juggling and spinning plates I guess.

So finally the only concern is my dojo.

Before the pandemic, I was able to hold small classes and private lessons there which paid the rent and some-times extra. Unfortunately I was now struggling to pay the rent let alone the excess. So this was my main concern hence being top of my list.

Coincidence or karma, I do not know, but the next day after I compiled my list, my friend Kam phoned and asked about the availability of the dojo. Kam already has it once a week which helps lower the bill that I owe him. The reason for the call was a friend of his, Dean, was looking for a premise to teach his students. We met and agreed on a charge, at the moment his rent pays mine so any lessons I teach are now profit – thank you book!

The next thing on my list was difficult as I was not quite

sure what exactly I wanted. I didn't want a full on relationship as I like living on my own, but I would like some female company when it suits me – I know I want my cake and eat it. Perhaps I have always wanted that. Anyway, one of the suggestions in the book is to join a dating site. This I was not sure about and did not really want to go down that road again. However, I thought I might dip my toe in the water with no expectations and see what turned up.

Almost immediately after I registered, I was contacted by a lady called Helima.

Helima was an Afghanistan lady who lived in Washington USA and was staying with her daughter in Shoreditch, London, when she contacted me. We spoke a few times and because she looked attractive and laughed a lot, I decided to meet up with her.

We arranged to meet at a restaurant near Liverpool Street. This suited both of us, it's easy for me to get the train and I am a bit of a train geek.

When arriving, obviously a bit apprehensive, I was pleasantly surprised as she looked better than her photos

and was pleased to see me. We sat talking for a couple of hours. She was good company and both tactile and complimentary to me. She said she could be my future wife, said she could not take her eyes off my lovely blue eyes and held my hand.

Of course I lapped this up, she was due to visit her cousin with her daughter and son-in-law but as she was having a better time than she had expected to, she called her daughter to arrange for her to come and meet her at the restaurant. I am only giving the backdrop to explain the immediate chemistry between us.

The following week I was bombarded with text messages and phone calls, a visit from her with her daughter and son in law. Looking back it does seem a bit surreal. On her visit we popped over to see my daughter and protector Lisa. Lisas comments were – she seemed lovely but be careful as she was a bit 'full on'. Helima was due to return to America at the end of the week and invited me over for Christmas and phoned me in tears from the airport. I got a message as she was boarding telling me how she was ' missing me already' and would contact me the minute she arrived.

Helima was good to her word, I got a message from her early hours the next morning saying

'I think I will pass'

With no explanation, I was confused, upset, shocked, all emotions. I don't wear my heart on my sleeve, but I needed to ask Lisa and some friends if I was missing some-thing.

No one could answer my questions. I did have a couple

of meet ups but there was no chemistry, only the bill. Seems a common factor, not even a hint of sharing the bill, oh Diana did offer. Still confused about Helima and boring my friends and students with the story to get other people's perspectives, I received a phone call from America, yes Helima!

I went straight for the juggler, what was going on!

Her response was classic – I read your autobiography on the plane and was distressed when I read some things about your past. How you burnt and tortured someone – I was twelve and burnt a boy at School with a magnifying glass! Also how you like the sound of breaking glass – again a boy with a catapult. However she said she could not get me out of her mind and was so sorry. We resumed our conversations more apprehensive this time but enjoyed our chats, she again invited me over and did mention a future. At this point I felt concerned. Things like when we were married and living in Washington slipped into the conversation from her. One time I had to cut the conversation short to go and collect a play kitchen I had bought on a market site for Esme, my granddaughter, for Christmas – this is relevant to the story. Helima asked, surprisingly out of context, about my financial situation. I explained that I manage to have an OK lifestyle, to go on holiday and asked about hers. She changed the subject "warning bells" not at the time. Not long after the conversation, I received a long message saying I am really sorry but I don't want to continue with this! Hope I am not upset and some tips: do not buy second hand presents for your grandchild, give her money towards a car. Esme is six! Also I should have bought her an ice cream when taking her and her family to Southend, she didn't mention the eighty pounds I spent on fish and chips, was it a scam? Did she have bi-polar? I will never know, just a coincidence that things changed after the financial conversation.

2023

Strange start, I am waiting for a shock treatment on my hip. I have had two hip replacements , probably due to my martial arts, but have suffered from bursitis. I have two steroid injections which only worked temporarily and was to go into hospital for shock treatment.

Mr Ranjid, my surgeon Mr Non-Charisma, suggested that I go to Orsett as it's the only place he does the small procedure. All the other ones had been in Worsley – a private hospital.

I was waiting to hear from the hospital when a call came through from Ireland. This man on the other end of the phone said he ran a private care company. He said there was up to a year's waiting list in Orsett and he could arrange for me to go into a private hospital and have the same procedure. He knew all of my information including my NHS number, doctor and surgeon. I explained that I had been informed that Mr Ranjid was the only person who performs this treatment in Orsett.

I contacted Mr Ranjid's secretary, who spoke to the hospital and came back and said that it was probably a scam.

What concerns me is how they got my information, were

they interjecting my emails or posts. But it did accelerate my visit to Orsett.

I am in constant pain and have a permanent limp and would be known as a snipers nightmare.

On the way home, I passed a house where Ron and Janice Chisam used to live. I have not seen Ron for possibly forty years.

Do I take a chance and knock at their door? Why not!

Ron answered and to say shocked was an understatement. Janice came over also looking shocked. They invited me in and I explained that I could not stay for as long as I was on my way to see Gary. We had a quick catch up and promised to meet up again. Again the reason for this part in the book is to endorse some of the stories I have written.Ron was at my being punched in the ear at Yarmouth and added about me having a fight with two people at the same time, whilst queuing for a burger. I had forgotten that one, then Janice added a couple of things that had happened some fifty years ago prior to her meeting Ron.

I had a couple of dates with her – she reminded me of my old Ford sit up and beg. The one where I took Janice out and she had to shine a torch through the windscreen as the lights were so dim. But the next part was even funnier. One Saturday morning, I went to Tilbury, not sure what for and was reversing when I hit a Volkswagen Beetle. I got out and apologised , it was totally my fault.

I had damaged this man's car and offered to give him ten pounds which he accepted and we shook hands.

That evening I went round to Janice's house to pick her

up to take her out. She lived in a town house in Chadwell St. Mary. Her parents were out whilst she was getting ready so I waited in the living room. Being nosey or curious, I was looking at the photos on the mantelpiece. Her Mum and Dad's wedding photo was there and I sort of recognised the man but I have a bad memory for faces. Something that is difficult as I know a lot of people so when people come up to me I ask generic questions like

'Are you still living in the same place?' Lisa always knows and gives me crafty looks when she is there and I think she has inherited the trait of not recognising people along with many others. Sorry Lis!

Anyway, back to the photos. Whilst waiting for Janice to get ready, her parents came home. Yes that's right – Janice's Dad was the man with the VW whose car I had hit. He had managed to repair the wheel hub and put it on the wall. So Janice joins the list of lucky escapes!

Out of the blue, Helima contacted me again, not once but 81 times. I only answered once to ask why , in this case it was me who had the lucky escape. Her messages were about when we get married she will buy my house that I rent.

I did have another lady contact me, although she said she was concerned with me being a Martial Artist and that I would probably only be interested in Athletic women, which she said she was not. Her photo showed her as attractive. I messaged her back and reassured her that I did not have a type and for me it was chemistry and humour that I found attractive. She thanked me for not being judgemental, she said she had put on a few pounds so did not have a slim figure. We had a chat and got on well, that was until she asked how tall I was. As I had made her feel better about her appearance I told her I was five foot eight. There was a silence before she informed me I was too short! That ended that conversation with the fat cow!!

Maxine, who I mentioned in the humour chapter, met me for a coffee and a catch up. I told her about the dating thing which I was a little embarrassed about, but she didn't seem surprised. Now I know why. She has four sisters. She told me she had gone to a family wedding with her Sisters and Brother when one of her Sisters was constantly on the phone. Maxine said

'Come on get off your phone we are supposed to be catching up'.

Her sister sheepishly replied that she was chatting to someone on a dating site and that Maxine may know the person she was speaking with, Maxine burst out laughing – it was me.

There will hopefully be a part two of this book if I'm still alive and kicking, well sort of with my dodgy hip and not a week that seems to go by without an incident!

As I have mentioned earlier in this book, it is not in any chronological order just when I think of things. Today is my Son Ian's 47th Birthday – what has this to do with my stories of gullibility you may ask.

Teresea was overdue with Ian in one of the hottest March on record unlike today when it is freezing. We were told that one way to induce labour was to go for a bumpy car journey. This may have been an old wives tale (where that expression comes from I do not know!) but back then I believed everything I heard, unlike now!

Well I drove down all of the bumpy roads I could find, not unlike today where a road without a pot hole would be more difficult to find. After about an hour and a half there was no sign of Teresea going into labour.

A car pulled out in front causing me to brake hard. If this did not accelerate the contractions what followed certainly did.

I don't normally use my horn but on this occasion I did.

The two lads then had the audacity to start swearing at me. I am not particularly intimidating to look at. I have a reputation that far exudes my capabilities and ventures but when the wrong button is pressed I do see a red mist. Lisa always says we have no amber lights on our traffic light system!

I think the two saw this and drove off rather rapidly.

Not long after Teresea went into labour and gave birth to my first child, Ian,

Whether or not this had anything to do with the almost immediate birth I do not know but it is a good possibility.

So the old wives tale should be amended to road rage not road trip brings on labour!

Being Jim

Summing up my life, would I change it, no! Success is measured by how far you have got with the talents you have been given. Do I trust too many people? Possibly.

Am I vain? A little. Who would have a stamp with his face on it.

Am I honest? Mostly

My passion in life is to help people to believe in themselves and to never let anyone bully or intimidate or belittle you. If a top surgeon did not have someone to empty his bins he would not be able to do his job. I often think of the honey bee and a flower analogy – they both need one another like comedians need audiences. I say these things because I don't like anyone looking down on another or on less fortunate people unless of course they deserve it and what I mean by that is if they don't try as if it's not the trying and failing it's the failing to try!

Printed in Great Britain
by Amazon

22371680R00106